WALKING
WITH
LONELINESS

WALKING WITH LONELINESS

Paula Ripple, F.S.P.A.

AVE MARIA PRESS   Notre Dame, Indiana

© 1982 by Ave Maria Press, Notre Dame, Indiana 46556.

International Standard Book Number: 0-87793-258-1 (Cloth)
                                     0-87793-259-X (Paper)

Library of Congress Catalog Card Number: 82-73048

Printed and bound in the United States of America.

Text design: Elizabeth French
Cover design: Katherine A. Robinson

FOR MY BROTHERS AND SISTERS
Juanita, Jack, Virgie, Mary Ann, Gordon,
Helen and Harold,
with thanks for your unconditional and
freeing love

Contents

Acknowledgments

With undying gratitude to my parents for the unshakeable vision of life that was their legacy.

In addition, I say thank you to:

My Franciscan Sisters whose love sustains and strengthens.

My friends in Guam, my second home, especially the young men and women at the Academy of Our Lady, Father Duenas Memorial School and Notre Dame High School. The energy of your love has been important in completing this manuscript.

Judy Gallagher who has been a faithful friend and a helpful secretary.

To all those whom I have met only through my books whose loving thanks have encouraged me to continue to write.

The Staff at the Paulist Center in Boston and the Paulist Fathers there for your care for me during my years in Boston.

I
A demanding companion

I think that what we suffer in this life can never be compared to the glory, as yet unrevealed, which is waiting for us. . . . We too groan inwardly as we wait for our bodies to be set free.

Romans 8:18, 23

Acquaintances and friends, poets and playwrights, artists and songwriters, the lettered and the unlettered all have one life companion that walks with them in a variety of ways and on very differing occasions. For some the companion seems only an aggravating and upsetting nuisance; for others, a challenging bearer of messages about life. Some seek to avoid the presence of this uninvited guest; others seek to better understand this companion's message. But, for all, the companionship of loneliness is a fact of life.

The presence of loneliness is more apparent at some times and in some lives than in others. In this way, loneliness is not unlike the reef that is visible from the dining room at Eastern Point Retreat House in Gloucester, Massachusetts. I have sat for hours and watched as the reef grows less and less visible with the incoming tide—until every one of the thousands of gulls perched on it has been forced to find a new resting spot. Then the tide changes and, ever so gradually, there is again a hint of land. Usually the gulls are the first to notice as they return to one of their favorite resting places. The reef is always there but its availability to the gulls and its visibility to me change with the movement of the water.

Some aspects of loneliness are for me like that reef. On some days and for reasons that are not clear to me, I am very much aware of some aspect of my own loneliness. In the presence of a friend or in doing something meaningful, I feel no loneliness, but once the friend leaves me or the task is completed, loneliness is again present to me.

Like the reef whose faces vary according to the position of the sun and the clouds, the presence of rain or snow, the coming and going of sea mist and fog, so too the faces of loneliness vary. It is not a single kind of experience if I think about it in some superficial way, but when I pursue the feeling and follow it, regardless of the face or form in which it began, it takes me to the same inner place.

The faces of loneliness that are reflected in the lives of friends and of other people whose lives I have taken seriously are sometimes the same and sometimes different from my own. It would be a tormentingly elusive companion were I to allow it to be so.

But, whatever its face or form, it is a companion for each of us. It is a companion that has evoked a variety of responses as people have discovered its unwelcome presence intruding on them and their lives.

Some ways that others perceive loneliness

Over the past months I have read several books, each dealing with loneliness from a different point of view. The titles of the books were, in themselves, revealing to me—titles such as *Escape From Loneliness* and *Loneliness: The Experience of Emotional and Social Isolation*. The treatment of loneliness was differentiated in a variety of ways such as "existential loneliness" and "anxiety loneliness," "primal loneliness," and "social loneliness."

As I looked into the works of the behavioral scientists, I was surprised to discover that the subject has been studied so little. For this reason, according to Frieda Fromm-Reichmann, we have no substantial theories about or understanding of loneliness. Sociologist Dr. Robert Weiss claims that "One of the burdens of loneliness is that we have so many preconceptions regarding its nature, so many defenses against its pain, and so little knowledge of how to help."[1]

There has been a general admission that the people who might be expected to know more about loneliness, even in terms of hard facts and data, do not have that information and offer differing explanations for their failure to pursue its meaning.

The use of the titles already cited and others I have noted in my own research in preparation for writing this book create the general impression that loneliness is of little value to human life in general and of no constructive value to the person walking in its companionship. Researchers Anne Peplau and Daniel Perlman state that, "Loneliness exists to the extent that a person's network of social relationships is smaller or less satisfying than the person desires." Weiss says, "The loneliness we have been told of is gnawing rather than ennobling, a chronic distress without redeeming features,"[2] and he further insists that he cannot agree with those who would speak of cherishing loneliness or who would treat it as a quest for a vision of life. This popular perception of loneliness as having no positive value may grow out of the little-understood nature of this ever-present human companion.

Others, in reflecting on loneliness, might speak of it as did the people of Austria who lived under Nazi rule and described those days as "a time without grace and a future without hope." It is not uncommon for us, when we are immersed in feelings of loneliness that seem overwhelming, to lose our ability to look beyond this moment, or even to believe that there is much beyond it. The suggestion that we enter into loneliness, there to discover its meaning, is not necessarily the one we want to hear. We might rather welcome some formula for release from its clutches.

In the light of this discussion and because of the painful and frightening experience that loneliness sometimes is, we hope to sketch a somewhat general stance that is observable when people confront their loneliness.

Young people run away from home to join religious cults and other groups claiming that they are lonely. Married people sometimes separate and divorce because they are terrified by the presence of this companion they never expected to pursue them in their marriage. Celibates have looked to marriage as a way to avoid the reality of loneliness. These examples and many others proclaim loudly the message that a good portion of the human race believes that loneliness must be avoided. Fleeing the companionship of loneliness has consumed vast amounts of human energy. It has given rise to escape syndromes that wear a variety of faces such as drugs, alcohol, violence in its many forms, abandonment of relationships, fear of entering into relationships, or building walls that create the illusion of making us less vulnerable.

It is as though we have been programmed by the songwriters, by novelists and poets, and even by psychologists and sociologists to believe that avoiding loneliness in whatever way is the best route to follow. Viewing loneliness as though it were indicative of some inherent personal weakness or of some lack in social skills leads necessarily to the common course of action known as running away from this aspect of life.

Loneliness as a challenging and life-giving companion

Loneliness is a companion whose presence has played a significant role in my life. I have walked with its constant and relentless presence, knowing it sometimes as an insistent prod and other times as a cajoling temptress. I have walked with it when its burden seemed heavy and when it gave rise to dancing feet and a song-filled heart. On some days I associate its presence with feelings of discouragement as the challenge appears too costly for me. On other days it gives rise to a desire to scale the heights and explore the depths in pursuit of its meaning. But, whatever the differences I have known, the surest thing for me is that loneliness is a companion I know well. And, though I understand its meaning less well than I might wish, I carry the conviction that its possible gifts are so great that to run away from it would be to reject constant offers of life.

Trying to unlock the meaning of loneliness has set me exploring the words of other writers, the songs that speak of it, and the stories that are important to me because of their many-layered meanings. The story that haunts me as I write is found in an old song of Bob Dylan's. The skeleton of the story that follows is his, the adaptation is my own.

The parable of the cave

In an ancient time the challenge of journeying to a place where one might find perpetual youth was widely known and followed. Equally sought after was an enduring wisdom. And so it was that three seers were encouraged to find what had been called the cave of wisdom and life.

They made careful preparations for what would be a challenging and arduous journey. When they reached the place of the cave they noted a guard at the entrance. They were not permitted to enter the cave until they had spoken with the guard. He had only one question for them, and he demanded that they answer only after talking it over with one another. He assured them that they would have a good guide to lead them through the regions of the cave. His question was a simple one, "How far into the cave of wisdom and life do you wish to go?"

The three travelers took counsel together and then returned to the guard. Their response was, "Oh, not very far. We just want to go far enough into the cave so that we can say that we have been here."

The response of the guard manifested none of his great disappointment as he summoned someone to lead the three men a short distance into the cave and then watched them set out again after a very short time, set out to make the journey back to their own land.

Loneliness and the parable of the cave

There is, for me, a feeling of disappointment that borders on having been betrayed by these three men. They made this journey in freedom and then bartered that effort in exchange for a superficial response. But such a response to life is not unique to them. It is an all too common way we all have of refusing to enter into those human experiences which hold for us the greatest meaning only if we are willing to pursue that meaning. Because we are free, it is sometimes too easy to run away from life at those very moments when life's call is the most costly and meaningful. It is too easy for us to walk toward the possibility of new and deeper life only to turn away when something tells us that to continue will lead us from familiar places into the unknown regions of our own heart and soul—there to discover and explore the rich spaces of new life for us.

There may be no human companion more challenging, no human experience more filled with the possibility of greater life than loneliness. In the deepest sense, there is a dimension of mystery to loneliness if we understand mystery to mean something that we can never fully comprehend.

And that each time we seek to comprehend, we do so at ever-increasing depths of meaning.

If we assume a stance toward loneliness that either denies or ignores its ability to lead us to fuller life, then we will also make it one of our life goals to escape its presence. We will invest energy in a non-productive process rather than using it in creative action.

If we approach loneliness only through the words and songs and reflections of others, we can never claim its meaning for ourselves. Like the three travelers we will repeatedly, through the beckoning of loneliness, come close to its touch and its embrace. Like them, we may turn from it at those most crucial moments—moments that are God's call to leave the security of the known and enter the insecurity of those who seek meaning in the foreign land that is the unexplored regions of human heart and soul.

If we approach loneliness as an inherently destructive force, or as a symptom of some human malady requiring clinical attention, we will look upon it as an affliction making us less than we are instead of perceiving it as a source of life.

We can make the same choice in relationship to loneliness that the three travelers made at the entrance to the cave. We can allow it to touch us in the least disturbing way and so close a door that wants to be opened wider.

It is unlikely that the three travelers forgot about their desire for wisdom, because it was a value to them. But it was a value for which they were unwilling to pay the price that risks all, to take the same risk that claims high stakes from us. It seems certain that, if we knew the story of the travelers from that point on, we would discover that they returned home and then set out on another and yet another journey, claiming to seek wisdom, but each time turning away from life at the most important moment. It is only at the point of risking all that we can claim faithfulness to the ever-pursuing call of a God who wants not just a little life for us but, as Jesus said, "life to the full." Following God's call to life present in our loneliness will lead us, as it did the man in Ezekiel 47, to walk into the waters of life to whatever depth we are willing to respond—ankle deep, knee deep, waist deep, or to risk all and walk even into waters that seem unsafe.

Loneliness and the persistent caller in the night

A young woman exclaimed to me recently, in the midst of tears and anger, "I did not ask to be lonely. I do not want to be lonely. I want to avoid it no matter what. So, how did it get into my life when I have worked so hard to avoid it?"

Loneliness is not something that we choose or fail to choose for our lives. It is a given for all of us. Its haunting and pursuing way is not unlike the story in Luke's Gospel and our response may well be like that of the once peaceful person asleep in the house.

> He also said to them, "Suppose one of you has a friend and goes to him in the middle of the night to say, 'My friend, lend me three loaves, because a friend of mine on his travels has just arrived at my house and I have nothing to offer him'; and the man answers from inside the house, 'Do not bother me. The door is bolted now, and my children and I are in bed; I cannot get up to give it to you.' I tell you, if the man does not get up and give it to him for friendship's sake, persistence will be enough to make him get up and give his friend all he wants."
>
> Luke 11:5-8

Loneliness for me is not *like* the "Hound of Heaven," it *is* God's presence, pursuing and calling us to life in ways we might never choose for ourselves because we might not otherwise be able to discover the most sensitive and delicate places from which new life can emerge.

Like the young woman for whom avoiding loneliness was such an important goal of life, like the travelers to the cave in search of wisdom who sought to escape its true cost, like the person asleep in the house who does not want to respond to the persistent caller, we have choices to make about our response. We must not choose to keep loneliness at a distance from our lives; it will not leave us at our bidding. Nor can we ever hope to leave it. It is at the center of the restlessness of the human heart.

We may tell ourselves that we can avoid it in much the same way that the three travelers believed that they could walk away from the challenge of entering into wisdom and life, preferring just to claim an association with it. Like the people who came to Jesus wanting only to touch him in order to be healed and then to return to their own lives, we sometimes want the jewel that is at the center of life without paying the personal price when the jewel we seek is wisdom or integrity, sensitivity or honesty, or the ability to give and receive friendship.

Loneliness is a part of the acquisition of every human value we wish to hold. It will lead us in ever deeper and more costly ways along that inward journey—a journey made into the deepest regions of the cave that is ourselves. Then we may return to those outside with an inner integrity out of which flows renewed life and a more profound hope.

My own life would not seem so lonely to me if I did not so often experience being torn between two worlds. Sometimes it seems to me that if I lived in a clearer world, a one-or-the-other world, it would be more simple and less painful. Instead, I find myself in a world that is often unclear, a world that is some of both worlds. To fear at once meeting and parting, being loved and being rejected, being cared about too much and not being cared about enough, seeing and not seeing, having someone too close and having someone too far away . . . these continual push-pulls challenge me and are costly for me. Something in me seeks greater certainty and clarity in much the same way that the person asleep in the house sought release from the persistent prodding of the night caller. Something in me also realizes that in seeking to avoid life-giving loneliness, I often choose it in a more lifeless form. Sometimes what seems to be the greatest loneliness really is not.

Lonely is . . .

1. To feel unloved

2. To feel a distance from a friend

3. To search for values

4. To have been hurt in loving

5. To see beauty around me and to have no one there with whom to share it

6. To feel that no one wants the gifts I have to share

7. To have lost a friend

8. A friend who challenges what I value

9. Meeting someone I was once close to

10. Making mistakes in loving

Much more lonely is . . .

1. To feel unlovable

2. To feel that there is no friend regardless of distance

3. To have no values and to want none

4. To hurt because I am unwilling to take the risk of loving

5. Not to see beauty around me

6. To believe that I have no gifts to share or to refuse to risk sharing them

7. Never to have taken the risk of having a friend

8. A friend who does not care enough to challenge me

9. Never having been close to anyone because I was afraid

10. Avoiding love so as not to make mistakes

11. Being in conflict with someone I love

11. Avoiding conflict with someone I love for fear of losing that person

12. Reaching out and having my hand ignored or rejected

12. Being unwilling to reach out for fear of rejection

13. When others do not like me

13. When I do not like myself

14. Being afraid of saying good-bye

14. Fearing to say hello

15. A broken dream

15. Removing myself from the possibility of dreaming

Loneliness and the foreign land of inner space

One of the painful realities of my own life is that while the feelings of loneliness that accompany me are gnawing and sometimes upsetting, their eventual impact on and the meaning for my life always unfolds gradually. At any given point in the actual experience, there is no discernible meaning present for me.

Though many have described loneliness as an energy or a force in human life, there are differing opinions about whether or not that force is destructive. My conviction is that whether loneliness is creative or destructive of my life depends on the choices I make in response to its presence. In this sense, it impacts on life much like suffering. The same kind of suffering through which one person grows and becomes more beautiful and loving can leave another hardened and embittered.

There is a dynamic tension at play (or at work) which reveals much of human life. Sometimes the moments of my greatest joy have also been times when some aggravating, gnawing hurt intruded. So, also, at moments of suffering, there have been spaces of great love given or great joy shared

with another. Opposites have a way of not seeing far from
one another.

It is not enough to notice life, important though that is. It
is also important for us to be open to that same life and to
enter into it with the faith that every opened door opens
other doors; every exploration of some unknown aspect of
our lives will inevitably call us to other unknown and life-
giving places. Part of the joy of this journey is discovering for
ourselves the once unknown in us. We will not do this if we
run away from that which is unpleasant or frightening, costly
or demanding. Along the way, we are like the Israelites, exiles
in some foreign land:

> By the streams of Babylon
>> we sat and wept
>> when we remembered Zion.
> On the aspens of that land
>> we hung up our harps,
> Though there our captors asked of us
>> the lyrics of our songs,
>> And our despoilers urged us to be joyous:
>> "Sing for us the songs of Zion!"
> How could we sing a song of the Lord
>> in a foreign land?
>>> Psalm 137:1-4 (NAB)

When we enter into those lonely spaces in our lives it is
not easy to sing and rejoice. As we walk with a measure of
uncertainty about the present, we may recall with fondness a
more certain past. We may live too much in the future as a
place of liberation. When we do this, we miss the graced moment of the present. It is at that moment that making the effort to "sing one of the Lord's songs" is important in much
the same way expressed in a song from *The King and I*:
"Whenever I feel afraid, I hold my head erect, and whistle a
happy tune, so no one will suspect I'm afraid . . ."

This has nothing to do with ignoring feelings or denying realities. Rather, it is a matter of the stance we assume when we are open to new life and when we are willing to give direction to our lives in response to God's ever-present call.

Loneliness and coming to greater insight

One of the surprising realities of life is the common experience of looking at something and thinking we have seen it. Then, upon looking at it later, we realize that we see it very differently from before. The reef, when it emerges, is somehow new and different.

This is true for us in looking at things, at people we meet, and at events. We may even ask ourselves the question, "Was this really what I saw before?" Or we may ask, "What has changed, myself or that at which I look?"—so difficult is it to comprehend what the experience means. When we try to verify what this means by talking it over with a person who shared both the first and the second experience, we may discover that both what the person saw the first time and sees now are totally different from what we saw, or believed we saw.

There may be an uneasiness in us about our changing perceptions. We may desire and seek greater clarity and greater certainty, believing ourselves to be unobservant or fitful in our seeing. We may even have some regrets and doubts about this human way of seeing one way and then seeing again differently.

While sharpening and sensitizing our ability to make observations is important, it is not so much seeing differently that is at the heart of the matter. Rather, our continual reflection on the noticing what is happening in ourselves can make the difference. St. Paul, in speaking eloquently of loving and sharing life with others, says:

> Now we are seeing a dim reflection in a mirror; but then
> we shall be seeing face to face. The knowledge that I have
> is imperfect; but then I shall know fully as I am known.
>
> 1 Corinthians 13:12

Paul's words are an invitation to us to accept the fact that this unclear way of seeing is a part of our humanness—a part to be accepted and cherished precisely because it is an ongoing challenge to be people of self-reflection; people who care enough about our lives to take them seriously and to notice what is happening in us and around us at any given moment. Jesus invites us to be pilgrims of the inner spirit who grow as we come to terms with an ever-changing vision of life. We see, we notice what we are seeing, we think about its meaning, we look and see again and in a different way, and so we grow to some new place.

This is a lonely way because we realize that we cannot rely totally on ourselves. No matter how many times we have made a journey like this one, we cannot trust that the vision or the meaning will remain the same. There is an insecurity about this way of living, this endless invitation to look and to see and then to look again and to see either more or less than the first time.

It is a lonely way because, as we look again, we may sometimes realize that something once dear is now less so or no longer so.

> Old paint on canvas, as it ages, sometimes becomes
> transparent. When that happens it is possible, in some pic-
> tures, to see the original lines: A tree will show through a
> woman's dress, a child makes way for a dog, a large boat is
> no longer on an open sea. That is called pentimento
> because the painter "repented," changed his mind. Perhaps
> it would be as well to say that the old conception, replaced
> by a later choice, is a way of seeing and then seeing again.
> . . . The pain has aged now and I wanted to see what was
> there for me once, what is there for me now.[3]

One of the precious gifts that loneliness brings is a discomfort or restlessness that can lead us to greater life, to greater vision and to keener awareness. Loneliness is a companion that does not want us to allow the best years of our lives to happen without us because we are present neither to ourselves nor to our lives.

Loneliness and growth to inner integrity

Through these pages I plan to offer no definitions of loneliness. I do not intend, either for myself or my readers, any final interpretations about its nature. There are some things I know from my own life and some that I have learned from the shared words and experiences of friends.

Loneliness is not a matter of who I am with or who I am not with; it is not a question, primarily, of presence or absence. Feeling lonely even when I am with someone I love, or feeling the presence of someone I love who is a continent away tells me this.

Loneliness is not a question of strength or weakness, or of psychological health. One of the common denominators for every person I know well is the companionship of loneliness present in their lives, however different their manner of walking with it.

Loneliness is not, of itself, an experience of isolation or desolation or of near despair. As costly as the loneliness in my own life has been, and as demanding as it has been in the lives of some people I greatly admire, its presence has continually led me beyond where I might have gone without its call.

I believe that loneliness is not, of itself, destructive. It is a creative energy that is a part of our humanness. It is an energy in us that is one of God's best gifts for our lives, for we are meant to grow in both our inner perceptions of our humanness and in our ability to share our human lives with one another.

What I do with loneliness makes a difference in the kind of person I can become. It makes a difference how I perceive loneliness and the stance I take toward it. It makes a difference whether I

—run away from it or enter into it

—look upon it as an evil or perceive it as a challenge

—ignore it or explore it

—see it as a personal weakness or limitation, or as a possible source of greater inner strength

—treat it as a problem or cherish it as a mystery

—fear it as God's way of punishing, or accept it as God's way of loving me to life.

My own life and the lives of others tell me that, at its deepest and most profound level, at that place where we find its true meaning, loneliness is related to our growth toward personal integrity. It is related to our ability to embrace and enflesh our own values and to live and walk with them. It is related to our ability to hold differing views, even from people who matter greatly to us, and to allow them to do the same. It is related to what some call "my ability to stand in my own place" and to take ownership of that place without compromise, even when it is questioned by someone, including a friend, who stands in a different place.

My own life and the lives of others tell me that our ability to be intimate with others, to share who we are without giving ourselves away, is centered in the lonely journey of self-discovery—when we have invested so well in that discovery that we can offer our gift without imposition, and receive the gift of another without desiring to remake that person into ourselves. The hidden expectations carried into relationships, and the manipulative giving that tries to bring another to the place where we stand because we are frightened by our differences, are related to Dag Hammarskjold's simple statement that "the longest journey is the journey inward." The companion for each of us all along the way is a feeling that we call loneliness.

Loneliness and the challenge of Jesus

As we pursue our search to find the meaning of loneliness and to unlock its mystery for ourselves, we seek switches to turn on the light in what sometimes seems like a darkness-only experience.

As we reach to find the courage that we need to make the inward journey, we do so not in isolation but as a people rich with the promise of God's own life waiting to be discovered.

As we walk with Jesus as friend and brother, we are reminded of those words of life which he left to us as costly heritage:

> The Pharisees and Sadducees came along, and as a test asked him to show them some sign in the sky. He gave them this reply: "In the evening you say, 'Red sky at night, the day will be bright'; but in the morning, 'Sky red and gloomy, the day will be stormy.' If you know how to interpret the look of the sky, can you not read the signs of the times? An evil, faithless age is eager for a sign, but no sign will be given it except that of Jonah."
>
> Matthew 16: 1-4 (NAB)

A "faithless age" knows the loneliness of the difficult and unanswered questions of life, and seeks an answer, a "sign" from Jesus. His response to us is a silent presence, a willingness to walk with us as we pursue those questions.

A "faithless age" knows the loneliness of pain and suffering and seeks from Jesus the removal of that pain. His response to us is in his presence with us in the Eucharist as he says, "This is my body broken; this is my blood poured out. As I have done, so I invite you to do."

A "faithless age" often stands in opposition to its own nature in its continual effort or expectation to be more than human and looks to Jesus to release us from the loneliness of the human condition. His response to us is in his willingness to let go of being only God to become the Word made flesh.

A "faithless age" grows weary of the insecurity and darkness which are a part of every person's life and seeks from Jesus the reassurance that it will never be dark for us.

A "faithless age" looks for signs, and Jesus says, out of the experience of his own human life, "The only sign you will be given is the sign of Jonah." The sign you will be given is the invitation to enter into the darkness of every human experience, not to remain there but to discover the light and life that is there. And, having discovered this light, to share it and life with others. This is the message of Jonah: Jesus entering into the darkness of Good Friday and all human darkness except sin, in order to share with us the fullness of human life. It is a reminder to us that the fullness of human life cannot be found at the margins of life, any more than the three travelers could find wisdom in its fullness without entering deeply into the cave.

The writers of the gospel do not speak directly of the loneliness of Jesus but we cannot miss the impact it must have had on his own journey if we look at the misunderstanding, rejection and betrayal that were a part of Jesus' life. Even his closest friends missed the meaning of the reason for his coming. They looked to him to be a person of power and earthly kingdoms despite all his words that this was not why he had come. The loneliness of Jesus must sometimes have been like the loneliness of one who has mastered a particular discipline to the point where it offers no new challenges. The loneliness of Jesus must sometimes have been like that of a person who has developed a finely tuned sensitivity to life and can rarely find someone with whom to share that feeling. The loneliness of Jesus must sometimes have been like the loneliness of the person who sees and tells the truth in the presence of people for whom truth is of less value than acceptability. The loneliness of Jesus was the loneliness of the individuals who have entered deeply into the cave of wisdom, of those who stand in their own place, of those of flawless inner integrity—as they relate to others who have lived as spectators rather than as participants, lived at the surface rather than at the depths.

Loneliness as a life-giving companion for us

I know what loneliness is. I have felt it in my body and in my heart. I have sometimes feared it, sometimes sought release from it, sometimes tried to ignore it or forget it. But, at those same moments, I have also never been far from the inner conviction that there was life for me in those dark spaces—life that pursued me with an intensity like no other.

I can speak of loneliness with authority only as it relates to me and to my life. I believe, because others have shared their lives with me, that their way of experiencing loneliness is not foreign to, nor is it different from my own way.

I can describe my feelings as I have experienced loneliness on the banks of the Mississippi and the Charles, on the shores of the Atlantic and the Pacific, in the inner city and in the small rural community. But, what I wish to center on is not so much how I have felt, as what I have done with the pain and the fearsomeness of those feelings, where I have allowed them to take me.

What I wish most to share is my own system for and manner of walking with loneliness. I wish to speak specifically of several people whose lives, because of some quality or facet, touched my own and made it possible for me to enter into my own journey. It is as though some aspect of the life of each of these persons has been an entry into the meaning of my own life as it was affected by loneliness.

I have come to terms with and made loneliness a manageable companion by trying to look at my life through the eyes and experience of others—persons who have been important to me as kindred spirits on the inner journey. Each person I have chosen to write about had some quality that caused me to believe that if they had been there with me, they would have understood and identified with my own feelings.

Reflecting on the role that each person has played in my life has been, for me, a source of inspiration. It has given me the courage and the good sense not to reject the companionship of loneliness but rather to find it at once challenging and probing, tender and life-giving. The messages of the lives of others reveal to me that often their most creative energies were, however mysteriously, set free in relationship to the very companion from which much of the human race seeks to escape.

Jesus could invite us to enter into the sign of Jonah, to enter into the darkness of life only because he had made the same journey. Jesus' challenge to us is to share in his experience, to find its meaning, so that we can experience our own lives more fully.

Like the three travelers to the cave of wisdom and life, we are called to find life's meaning not in isolation but in sharing our experiences, by entering deeply into our own lives, and by sharing the depth of experience that has been a part of another's life.

We can taste the fullness of life only if we do not refuse the final piece of the road which leads us through loneliness to the fullness of human life that is always revealed when we pursue life and God's call to it with the same ardour that God pursues us:

> I think that what we suffer in this life can never be com-
> pared to that glory, as yet unrevealed, which is waiting for
> us. The whole creation is eagerly waiting for God to reveal
> his sons. . . . From the beginning till now the entire crea-
> tion, as we know, has been groaning in one great act of
> giving birth. . . . We too groan inwardly as we wait for our
> bodies to be set free.
>
> Romans 8:18-19, 22-23

Through the companionship of loneliness, life has been revealed to me. In its companionship I have found both hope and happiness. Because of the journey on which my loneliness has led me, I have discovered worlds inside and outside of me that I may never otherwise have found. My own loneliness has led me down intense paths of searching for meaning that I would neither have chosen nor pursued for myself. My loneliness demanded I look deeper and farther and beyond myself. My loneliness has led me into the lives of others, people close to me, others I have met only briefly, and some I have never personally met—searching to understand how they had walked with this ever-present and persistent in-viter to life.

The messages of these life companions have been sources of hope and courage. Their ways of inspiring and strengthen-ing me would probably surprise each of them, for they might not have seen the meaning in their lives that I have. It is like a poem that has a meaning for the reader that it did not have for the writer.

Sharing my companions on this journey with you may invite you to greater attentiveness to your own inward journey, and so enrich the journey as you seek to share it in each friendship.

1. *Psychology Today*, October 1979.
2. *Loneliness: The Experience of Emotional and Social Isolation*, Robert Weiss, ed. (MIT Press).
3. *Pentimento*, Lillian Hellman (New Signet).

II
Naming our days and owning them

Do not be afraid, for I have redeemed you;
I have called you by your name, you are mine.
Should you pass through the sea, I will be with you;
or through rivers, they will not swallow you up.
Should you walk through fire, you will not be scorched
and the flame will not burn you.
For I am Yahweh, your God,
the Holy One of Israel, your savior.
. . . Because you are precious in my eyes,
because you are honored and I love you. . . .
Bring back my sons from far away,
my daughters from the end of the earth,
all those who bear my name. . . .

Isaiah 43:2-7

An experience of loneliness common to all of us is the death of someone we love. There is a cruelty in death in how it separates us from the touch and the voice of another so that we miss the person more, not less, with each passing day.

The death of another, especially someone we love, carries with it an urgent invitation to notice how we are living, how we are responding to our own selves, our friends and our days. So it was with my mother's death for each of her eight children. And so it might have been my mother's prayer that Isaiah formed: "Bring back my sons and my daughters from the end of the earth, all those who bear my name. . . ."

There is a mystery about the reality of death, a mystery that carries a unique quality. Death is a human experience which has no meaning of its own. Death takes all of its meaning from life. We know this when we stop to think about wakes and funerals that we have attended. Once the details of the death are reviewed, the conversation immediately turns to the life of the deceased.

We know that the meaning of death is related to life when we recall that in those last moments of life, dying persons speak of life—speak of those things which have been most important during the days of their lives. Jesus, on the cross, spoke of forgiving as he prayed even for his tormentors, spoke of caring as he invited his mother and his best friend to care for each other, spoke of hope as he offered a message of promise to a hopeless criminal dying on a cross next to him.

In their last moments, parents speak to their children of those same things which preoccupied their lives. It is the last opportunity to review the fabric of their lives. It is a last opportunity to reveal who they are most and what values are most important for their lives—so important that others are invited to listen carefully and to emulate and so to grasp hold of their own lives.

I deeply regret that I was not present for the death of either my father or my mother. I wish that, somewhere in my memory, I had the treasure of their final words so I could recall them as I reflect on the meaning and direction of my own life. Since I do not have that memory, I seek to remember the days of my mother's and my father's lives, and to notice how they themselves were present to those days which were their lifetimes.

My mother and I talked about her death long before her dying. When we did, she reviewed her life with me. She told me about some of her happiest days and about some of her lonely ones. She talked about my life as she saw it.

She reminded me of how important it is for me to notice the kind of person I am and the kind of person I choose to be.

Our conversations brought to my mind some favorite words of Herb Gardner's play, *A Thousand Clowns*, and I told my mother that he described being present to life as "naming our days and owning them." My mother said she liked that way of thinking about it and believed she had tried to live that way. It was clear to me that my mother's life had not happened without her. It was also clear that her loneliest moments, as she described them, were times when others did not seem to understand her decisions about how she had "named her days."

During those conversations I told her that, if my other brothers and sisters agreed to it, I wanted to offer some final message about her. And so it was that, when I came home to be with my family at the time of my mother's death, I asked my three brothers and four sisters what they most remembered about mother's life. Together, then, we might remember her in a way that she would want to be remembered. I wanted to remember her in a way that was not larger than her life, but lifelike.

I had jotted down notes on a cross-country flight, notes that spoke of what I most remembered. I tried carefully to avoid sharing my notes until I had asked all of my brothers and sisters what they most remembered about her. It is a marvelous testimonial to my mother that the eight of us who had seldom agreed about anything as children, who still have our differing perceptions of life, should have agreed so about what we most remembered and wanted to say to her and about her.

My mother, until after my father's death, would never have spoken of herself as a lonely person. It might make little sense for me even to suggest that a woman who had a husband and eight children could claim even one lonely day in her life. But it makes good sense to me. No person comes to be the kind of woman that my mother was without walking through the demanding and costly pilgrimage of a lonely inward journey. Even as a child I noticed my mother's dependence on my father for some things, yet her strong and clear personal identity was also obvious. This sense of self made it possible for her to be present to a husband and eight children, each vastly different, though clearly children of the same parents. Coming to be that kind of person does not just happen. It is the result of coming to know one's own name as God knows it; it is also the result of naming one's days and giving direction to them.

As a child, I would not have thought about how loneliness was for my mother. But when my mother and I came to know one another not just as mother and daughter but as friends, she told me about those places and ways in which she walked with her loneliness. Always it was related not to where she was or who was with her; rather, it was more a part of her search for values and for herself as her vision of life may have differed from that of her own brothers and sisters, her children, or even of my father.

She was a woman well aware of the cost of living. She was present to both life's deepest joys and its greatest concerns. Perhaps one of her most important gifts to her children was that she challenged us, in large ways and in small, to develop that same kind of awareness of life so that the best years of our lives were not happening without us. Presence to life was high on her list of priorities—for herself and for us.

For my mother, being present to life meant being aware of a threefold presence in her life. The home and family from which I come would not be looked upon as "religious" or "pious" as religion and piety are often proclaimed. There was little specific God talk in our home. My mother's kind of religion was an ongoing awareness of the presence of God, linked with the conviction that God is far from us if we are not present to one another and to ourselves.

She also knew that presence to others was not measured by an abundance of theoretical concepts about what it means to care for others. It was measured, rather, by all the practical and daily ways in which she offered the warmest kind of hospitality to others. As a child growing up, I can remember few times when there was not someone living in our home, a guest who came to visit and was invited to stay on. Most often, it was someone we did not know well but who had some special need at that time.

I believe that my mother was present to others because she knew who she was. My mother "knew her name" in ways that God knew it. She knew it so well that, when God called her on that day in May, she was a part of naming the day and the hour even as she had named all the days of her life with thoughtful care.

Naming and owning our days

As I thought about what I wanted to say at her funeral, I remembered some words in a *Dictionary of Biblical Theology* about what the concept of naming meant in the Hebrew scriptures. Two passages came to mind: "For the ancients naming is not simply a conventional designation, but rather an expression of a being's place in the universe," and "since the name is the person himself, to do something about a name is to have a hold on the being."[1]

These phrases fit exactly my sense of how my mother lived her life. They explained for me why "naming her days and owning them" was a costly and sometimes lonely process. They helped me understand that, for myself as for my mother, coming to know my own name and naming the days that God gives to me are something that I do in relationship to others but must also do for myself.

That favorite passage from the play *A Thousand Clowns*

that I talked with my mother about also came to mind. It seemed like a perfect work within which to build my own and my brothers and sisters' memories of our mother.

> "Oh, Arnie, you don't understand anymore, you got that wide stare people stick in their eyes so nobody'll know their head's asleep. . . . The only thing you got left to reject is your food in a restaurant if they do it wrong and you can send it back to make a big fuss with the waiter. . . .
>
> "Arnold, five months ago I forgot what DAY it was. . . . I'm on the subway on my way to work and I didn't know what day it was and it scared the hell out of me. . . . I couldn't remember, I didn't know, unless I really concentrated, whether it was Tuesday or Thursday . . . or a . . . for a minute . . . it could have been any day, Arnie . . . sitting in the train going through any day . . . in the dark through any year. . . .
>
> "Arnie . . . you have to know what day it is. You got to know what's the name of the game and what the rules are with nobody else telling you. You have to own your days and name them, each of them, every one of them, or else the years go right by and none of them belong to you. . . ."[2]

As I thought about how my mother had named her days and owned them, I realized that it will not matter if I name my days differently from hers. What does matter is that faithfulness to God and to myself demands that I name each one, as each person who is a part of this book has done.

To "name our days" is to be in charge of our lives. I can think of no one whose life has mattered greatly to me, in whatever way, who was not making this same effort to express their "place in the universe" and to "have a hold on that being" that was theirs. For each of them, faithfulness to this effort was marked by loneliness.

Some of the names my mother gave to her days

Reviewing with my brothers and sisters what we most remembered about my mother and her life was, for each of us, a time of personal inventory and fond remembering. Reviewing my mother's days made us keenly aware that she would not have been so introspective about all of this. She might not even understand exactly why all this matters so much to me.

This is a reminder to me that what we are talking about here is more a question of a way of life than of individual actions and choices. It is a reminder that we make these choices not to be noticed by others or so that others can give names to our days. Precisely because the notice of others would not have mattered to my mother, the difference that it makes, in the end, is all the greater. Reviewing how she named her days evoked in me an attentiveness to my own life.

Self-sacrifice is neither a well-known nor widely acclaimed quality in our time. We live in an age that looks upon self-fulfillment as one of its hallmarks. I never heard my mother use either of these expressions because self-sacrifice was woven into the fabric of her life, and self-fulfillment was its natural outgrowth.

So instinctive was her giving of herself that it had no self-referencing qualities. Her giving was done with the sort of graciousness that left her children and others with the feeling that we had done her a favor in receiving. I believe that her giving had integrity because my mother was not a compulsively self-sacrificing person. She was able to receive with equal ease, allowing those who knew and loved her to be there for her in the same ways in which she was present for them.

There was an effortlessness in her manner of approaching life. It remains a mystery to me how a woman who was so responsible for an "army of ten" regenerated the loving energy which seemed inexhaustible and boundless. It would be too simple to quote the half-truth that says, "It is better to give than to receive," or even the lovely words of Francis, "For it is in giving that we receive." The surest thing I know is not how my mother was able to give so much but that she did it. And because she did it so well, self-sacrifice is a way of naming my days that is a value for me. Unlocking the secret of how I can learn to give as she did is helped by the good gift of my memory of her.

Freedom is a frequently used word today. Freedom and the rights of the individual are at the heart of much that goes on in both the streets and the courts. What I sometimes forget—something my mother never seemed to forget—is that real freedom is a matter of the inner spirit. My mother's inner freedom manifested itself in many ways, but there is one way that stands out among all the others.

Because my mother was free inside, she who had given life to eight children never took back the life she gave. There are parents who believe that their children are their property. There are parents who give life to their children on the day of birth and then take that life back each day so that a child at 20 is less free than at two. There are parents who do not allow their children to name their days.

My mother gave us life and was attentive to our lives so that we had freedom enough for mistakes and for learning. Out of her own sense of freedom she called us to accountability and to responsibility in a way that a free and freeing love does.

Friends who offer love to one another must also give the freedom friendship needs to grow. Friends sometimes claim ownership in destructive ways. Friends must allow space for naming and owning days.

I do not remember my mother ever offering eloquent

words on the value of personal freedom for herself or others. I do know that her finely tuned sense of personal freedom made of her a woman who offered love without control and invited responsibility without dictating. That memory of her has called me to be attentive to how I stand in relationship to others.

Faithfulness will be a forgotten word in the 21st century unless we are aware of the subtle and persistent influence that tries to tell us that faithfulness is not possible. Little in our lives consistently reminds us of the value of fidelity. Today, words like liberation and human rights are valued in a way that distorts the fullness of life for all. There is much talk about freedom from, but little emphasis on freedom for. Reflected through the media and in the lives of many people in our "free" culture is a casualness about relationships and the destructive ways we enter and leave them without ever asking what we are saying when we say hello or good-bye.

Unless we have paid the personal price of being faithful to ourselves, unless we have at least entered into that lonely inner journey which will lead us to love and care for ourselves, it is not likely that we will offer love and care to others. It is not likely that we can offer faithfulness to a friend unless we have discovered the meaning and the value of being faithful to commitments that we have made to ourselves.

My mother's faithfulness, to a casual observer, might be seen in her faithfulness to her husband and to her children. And that would be one important way if one were measuring. But she revealed the value she placed on faithfulness to herself when she shared with me some of the ways in which differences in her own family had been costly for her as a young woman. She told me, for example, what it had been like for her to be the wife of a public school superintendent in a small town with all the political pulls on both her and my father, and she reminded me of the ways in which differences among her own children had sometimes been painful for her.

The last summer my mother was alive we were having one of our long chats and, still nourishing the freedom of her children, she inquired about my own happiness as a member of a religious community. She told me then something I had never known. She told me that my father never wanted me to enter my order because he believed that the oppressive rules of that time might break my inner spirit. Neither my father nor my mother had ever given any hint of that, so careful were they for our freedom to choose what our futures would be, so profound was their example of faithfulness to life.

Because it is only in that environment of freedom that one can grow and grow up, because it is only when the love of another is freeing that we can choose to be faithful, I have come to cherish the example of faithfulness of which my mother spoke through her life.

The great era of celebration in which we live both in the church and in a rainbow-balloon-decked world, was instinctive in my mother. Birthday parties for each of us, great family feasts, and the centrality of the kitchen in our home, all proclaimed clearly, in ways the theology of the Eucharist once did not, that every meal we shared was sacred and was somehow related to going to Mass together on Sunday.

My mother did not speak of the importance of parties. She was just instrumental in making them for every and all sorts of occasions—complete with decorations for the house and the table, complete also with whatever strangers she sensed needed an invitation.

One of the greatest realizations for my life, as I saw my mother growing old, was that she was all of and more of the good things she had been through all her life.

And so it was with her sense of celebration. In the later

years of her life, she rested when she needed to, but she never missed a party.

My mother's life was not one huge celebration. How could it have been with a large family, moving frequently to be where my father's work took him, and all of life's usual circumstances? All the more reason to notice the inner strength out of which she chose to retain a certain attitude toward life that could have been quite different if she had chosen to be a complainer instead of a celebrator. My mother was a person who believed that there is light in every darkness if we look for it, and that it is not so much what life brings to us as what we bring to it that will determine the names our days bear to others.

How my mother retained a firm commitment to personal prayer is somewhat of a mystery to me. In a home for ten (plus a visitor or two) there is always something to be done, someone's tears to be dried, some school function to attend, some preparation needed for the next meal. As a child, I was taught to pray, my parents prayed with me, but I never thought about when my mother prayed. I know she must have, for even surviving with eight children could be looked upon as monumental. My mother did better than that—she enjoyed her family and loved us. That is one of my clearest memories.

My mother shared many of her secrets with me during the last several summers I visited her. One of the things she and I would do at least once but often several times each day was to pray the rosary. I wonder now how many times her fingers made their way around those beads during the last years of her life.

After the rosary, often during a walk, she taught me about prayer in ways she understood it and did it. She spoke of its importance to her through all her life, but especially, in the years since my father's death. My mother's name was Mary and when I think of her now I think of Luke's words, "Mary treasured all these things and reflected on them in her heart" (Lk 2:19, NAB).

The days of my mother's life clearly belonged to her. She had named them and so she owned them. Because they were hers, she could hand them on to us not as givens for us but as goals for which to strive. She could offer them to God because she had walked the sometimes lonely way through which a person claims her own name and then is allowed by God to name the day of her death, as I believe my mother did.

Life as it is reflected through death

Death is that reality which takes its meaning from life. We understood, through my mother's dying, the meaning of her life in ways we had not reflected on while she was still alive. A gift she gave us was that she had been so attentive to life that her death brought us to greater attentiveness to our own lives and to a greater love for hers.

I am sure my mother never saw this slogan from an old airlines ad, but she lived its meaning: "Don't let the best years of your life happen without you." Because my mother was present to her own life, she could be present to us. Because she was present to her life, she gave us an example of living our own lives that way. The names she gave to her days matter to us now. They are a continual reminder to name and own our own days as her children.

Sometimes people are urged to prepare for death in the words of St. Paul:

> That is why it is said,
> "Wake up, sleeper,
> and rise from the dead!
> And Christ will shine on you."
> So pay close attention to how you live.
>
> Ephesians 5:14 (GNB)

My mother had paid close attention to how she lived. Because she was present to her life, she was ready for the call: "Do not be afraid, Mary, for I have redeemed you. You are precious in my eyes, you are honored and I love you."

Because she had named her days and owned them, she could hear her eight children saying, "Thanks, Mom, for caring enough. . . ."

1. *Dictionary of Biblical Theology*, Xavier Leon-Dufour, S.J. (New York: Desclee, 1967).
2. *A Thousand Clowns*, Herb Gardner (New York: Random House, 1961).

III
Rebuilding broken dreams

For there is hope for a tree,
if it be cut down, that it will sprout again,
and that its shoots will not cease.
Though its roots grow old in the earth, . . .
yet at the scent of water, it will bud
and put forth branches like a young plant.
Job 14: 7-9 (RSV)

We read in the book of Proverbs, "Without a vision the people perish" (29:18). Indeed, without a dream the people die.

God's word is filled with the human stories of dreamers who listened carefully to their own lives and so discovered God's dream for them. For them God's word was rich with the promises of life which only he could at once offer, and then fulfill when they were faithful.

Like the early Followers of the Way, God calls us to be a people who dream, a people whose dreams are never completely fulfilled. God's word for us, as it was for them, will not be a way of explaining either the dream or our lives, but an invitation to catch hold of and then live God's dream. We are a people called to risk, not to security. We are a people who must sometimes lose in order to find, who must sometimes be lost before we can be found.

Like the early Followers of the Way we are called to be a people who continually choose new dreams, give new life to old ones, let go of broken ones. Grasping and living God's dream for us is a journey, however, that can be fearsome and lonely. To respond in faithfulness we will need companions who nourish and share one another's dreams.

"Without a vision the people perish" is a message heard

by people of all ages and cultures. It is not for the faint-hearted, but for those with a strength that is God's own. It is not a message for those who cling to the security of the known. In order to discover some new place of life, we must leave the familiar and the comfortable and enter into the unfamiliar and the uncomfortable—a place that can be lonely.

The message of the lives of other dreamers who trusted God's promise of life even when they did not understand all of it, perhaps offers us the most comfort as we seek to follow God's dream for us. The loneliness of the journey is less frightening when we remember the lives of other dreamers who walked with God.

The practical ones of the world look to logic and to plausible explanations. The dreamer pursues God's own folly and trusts when reason alone is put aside for a message that calls from some deeper place of unfolding life. To believe in dreams is to believe in more than we could dare to hope for and to do so without reasons. To believe in dreams is to believe in life because we believe in the author of life whose wisdom unfolds in human dreams that are pursued with openness and with courage. This way of living was expressed by Rainer Maria Rilke:

> I believe that almost all our sadnesses are moments of tension that we find paralyzing because we no longer hear our surprised feelings living. Because we are alone with the alien thing that has entered into our self; because everything intimate and accustomed is for an instant taken away; because we stand in the middle of a transition where we cannot remain standing. For this reason the sadness too passes; the new thing in us, the added thing, has entered into our heart, has gone into its inmost chamber and is not even there anymore—is already in our blood. And we do not learn what it was. We could easily be made to believe that nothing has happened, and yet we have changed, as a house changes into which a guest has

entered. We cannot say who has come, perhaps we shall never know, but many signs indicate that the future enters into us in this way in order to transform itself in us long before it happens.[1]

As we are dreaming our dreams, we are already being transformed by them. As we share them, we help transform one another's lives. As we share them, we are released from the loneliness along the way.

It is important for us to remember the dreamers whose lives have taught us about both the gift and the cost of being dreamers. It is in the message of the lives of others that we find important keys to continue fashioning new dreams and to let go of broken dreams.

—Moses had a dream of freedom for his people. It was a dream that was more costly than he could have known when he embraced it. Scarcely had the waters of the Red Sea come together again when his people began to complain that they had been better off in Egypt. They doubted his dream, wondered why they had exchanged one wasteland for another. And Moses' faithfulness to his dream was tested.

—Jeremiah had a dream that a desolate land would again be a place of life and that vineyards would again grow. People ridiculed and laughed at him as Jeremiah pursued his dream.

—Ruth had a dream when she believed that by her faithfulness to Naomi others might break out of the narrow and confined meaning of generous love. It was a costly dream because it separated her from her homeland. Yet, she followed the dream.

—Francis of Assisi had a dream that a church allied with the regal and the powerful would again be faithful to itself and its mission. Some laughed at this simple man whose dream seemed so large, whose dream grew out of his call to "rebuild the church."

—Pope John XXIII had a dream of a church restored and healed of its unfaithful ways, a church renewed from the inside out. And there were those who sought to thwart this dream.

—Dag Hammarskjold had a dream of a world community in which the emerging and powerless nations would be helped and nourished through various forms of aid. He sought a world community where the rich would no longer exploit the poor. And some sought to end his dream when he was murdered in Africa on a mission of peace.

—Martin Luther King had a dream in which men and women would reach across the differences that separate—differences of sex, of race, of creed, of education and culture. His dream did not die with him.

—Mother Teresa has a dream that every person will know, before they die, that they are loved. Her dream continues.

—Archbishop Romero had a dream that his people would be free from the slavery of being poor and powerless. His enemies sought to wrest that dream from him just after he had spoken the sacred words, "This is my body for you" and "This is my blood given for you," after he had broken wide the message of God's word.

One dreamer's life links all of us who bear the name Christian. He is the Man of Galilee, he is Joseph's son, this man of whom some asked, "What does he know, this carpenter's son?" We must listen most closely to his life if we wish to follow God's call to fashion and follow our dreams. His life is the only one substantial enough for us if our dreams are to be life-giving and farseeing. Of his dream, more than all others we might say, "Without this dream and this dreamer's life, the people perish; without the message of this dreamer's life, the people die." His was the greatest dream for each of us, "I have come that you may have life, life to the full" (Jn 10:10).

Our following that dream of Jesus is not merely a question of fashioning new dreams, for costly as that is, the signs of hope and new life are present. The measure of our commitment to Jesus' dream for us is in rebuilding broken dreams in the same way that he did as he was led to his own abandonment and death. The test of the faithful follower of Jesus is in our belief in the paschal mystery. It is in our willingness to walk into and then through our own dying until we come to our own day of rising. It is in our willingness to hand over our broken dreams as Jesus spoke of handing over his own spirit and then, like him, to claim a new spirit present in a refashioned dream.

The task of rebuilding broken dreams is lonely because it places us in a position of insecurity. When we have walked some distance with a dream that has been ours it becomes a familiar place of life. To enter into the search for new life, to seek to refashion a life dream, puts us between what has been and that which is not yet. It leaves us with no secure resting place and calls us only to risk and vulnerability. To pursue the dream, to accept the lonely price of discovering the new life, is not something we can do by and for ourselves alone.

The keys to refashioning broken dreams

Fortunately for us, the first of these keys is God's pursuing love and care for us. Because the dream we follow is God's own dream for us, because the full life we seek is God's gift to us, the promise of his presence is unquestionably faithful. We need only seek to remove those obstacles in ourselves which prevent us from accepting and entering into companionship with a God who is like a warm and loving environment. We need only to notice God's presence with us in ways we sometimes do not. God is the only presence in our lives that can at once call us to life and then give us the gifts necessary to follow that call. God is the only presence in our lives who at once offers the dream and then fulfills it in us if we are free of the obstacles that would prevent the dream from coming to reality.

The second key remains, in most of us, largely un-discovered or unacknowledged. It is the key of the endless goodness and giftedness that is in each of us. A God who loves us has given us countless gifts. I believe with Teilhard de Chardin that God has made of each of us "an irreplaceably precious gift." The journey of life, the lonely inward journey, must be made in order to discover the goodness that is in us. Unless we believe that this gift has been given to us by a God whose love is so generous, we may never make this journey. We might fear that we might not like ourselves if we really came to know who we are.

And so, the third key becomes vital to our lives. If we are to discover and believe in the first two keys, we must know that we will never do that in isolation from other people. Baptism is the sacrament of companionship, it is a sacrament calling us to make the human journey in the companionship of others. In isolation from others, we will not cling to the belief in God's presence nor to the desire to search for the goodness in ourselves. A healthy sense of our ability to sin need never hide from us the conviction that there is more goodness and gift in us than we will ever discover. It will only be revealed to us as we seek to give and receive love in response to God's call to us to be friends.

The third key is functional for us only if we are nourished by the bread for the journey which is the Eucharist. Only if, as friends, we meet and share life at the table to which God calls us and calls us to be friends to each other.

Finally there is a fourth key. We need the presence of some individuals whose quality of life and whose manner of searching holds out to us the human hope that, like them, we can follow even when the call is unclear and the way unknown. We need the clarity of the lived example of others who did what we know we must do as we leave the certain for the uncertain place of life.

Through all my life I have needed and looked for messages in the lives of others who had some meaning for my own life. As a Christian, I have found those messages first in the life of Jesus and then in the lives of figures in the Hebrew scriptures and in the gospels. I have reflected on the meaning of the lives of some of the saints with whom I seemed to share life questions.

But all of this is given flesh and blood for me only if I can relate it to someone living here and now. Each time I have walked through the pain of some broken dream of my own I have had my eyes and my heart fixed on some person with whose life I could identify in some important way.

There are many people whose way of living some aspect of their lives has made a profound difference to me, people whose commitment to their own journey inward has helped me to continue my own. Many of them not only survived but grew through some personal tragedy. Each of them came to some new place of greater life.

I remember the first time I heard a Vietnam veteran named Max Cleland speak. From him came powerful words about the cost of losing an energetic and even robust body and returning home a triple amputee. He returned home not to a hero's welcome, but to the severest kind of criticism for having been part of an unpopular and unsupported war. I cannot forget his impact as he spoke of the feelings he had to deal with—his loneliness because so few could understand. Cleland embodies a quotation from Ernest Hemingway in *A Farewell to Arms*: "Life breaks us all sometimes, but some grow strong at the broken places."

The challenge of Max Cleland's life stays with me as a reminder to notice when and if I am growing strong through the brokenness that is a part of my life.

I think with gratitude of the gift a lovely woman named Lillian brought into my life and into the lives of many people. Having come through the traumatic process of divorce, she was injured in another equally tragic event to find herself paralyzed and confined to a wheelchair. Her response to both of these broken dreams was to find new life for herself and to become actively involved in sharing that life with others who had to search for a new dream in the ways she had. Her refusal to allow herself to be broken by her broken dreams continues to give me courage and hope.

A dreamer named Terry Fox

The message of their lives is very close for me to the life of a young man who clearly knew that without a dream he would die. I first met him when I went to Brockville, Ontario, in September of 1980. The weekend I has there, the front page of every paper in Canada carried the story, "Terry Fox collapsed today in Thunder Bay," and the question hidden in each story was, "Will the Marathon of Hope end there?"

Terry Fox was a young man who, at age 19, had lost a leg to cancer. With it he lost many of the dreams a young man has for his future. The stories written about him reveal his own sadness and disappointment; they reveal the humanness of his "Why me?" question and his temptation to bitterness.

But, most of all, they reveal the quality of the life deep inside him because, while he was still in the hospital, he began to fashion what he later called the Marathon of Hope. Having experienced his own hurt, he concluded that not only for himself but for others, "Somewhere the hurting must stop." He also concluded that he would do his part for others who had suffered from cancer as he had. He wanted to help others who might not have had the help and the care he had received from his family and friends, and the medical people. Terry wanted to grow strong so he could run across Canada to share the dream he had for his own life and for others. He believed in both the wisdom of dreaming and in the possibility of new life:

> For there is hope for a tree
> if it be cut down, that it will sprout again,
> and that its roots will not cease.
> Though its roots grow old in the earth, . . .
> yet at the scent of water, it will bud
> and put forth its branches like a young plant.
>
> Job 14:7-9 (RSV)

With the cooperation of the Canadian Cancer Society and with the support of the people of Canada, Terry pursued his dream. The dream was tested on September 2, 1980, when he collapsed in Thunder Bay. It was discovered that the cancer had now spread to his lungs. Terry was flown home to British Columbia.

I returned to Canada in June of 1981 and friends there gave me a copy of the *Terry Fox Story* which a reporter named Leslie Scrivener had written around the journal that Terry had kept while he was running. I spent most of my return flight, with tears in my eyes, reading of the courage of a young man who might have given up on life.

Later that night I finished reading the book and then turned on the late night news to hear that Terry Fox had died that night. Of Terry the newscaster said, "The simplicity and beauty of Terry's dream fascinated and inspired the people of Canada. He transformed our nation with his dream. It was the dream of a young man innocent enough to believe he could make the world a better place and a young man wise enough to do it modestly." Another said that "Terry was uncommonly blessed with hope. His hope is a gift that is his heritage to the people of Canada."

The keys to Terry's life-giving journey through his own broken dreams are readily available in his spirit and in his words. It is inconceivable to me that anyone could read his story and listen to the message of his spirit without finding renewed hope and the courage to pursue one's own life purpose.

Many qualities about his life come to my mind and there are many feelings in me as I review why he made such a difference to me as I try to deal with my own broken dreams. A few stand out among these. It is these qualities that are like that "scent of water" of which we read in the book of Job. Without them, new life might not have appeared for Terry. Without them, new life would be more difficult for me.

—Though he accepted and entered into his own pain, that was not enough for him. In and through his own pain, he cared about the suffering of others. All across Canada, as he ran, Terry stopped to spend time with children who were also victims of cancer. He wanted the hurting to stop not only for himself but for others.

—He believed that even in our complex world one person's dream does matter. He wanted others to believe that for them as for him, what we do with our lives makes a difference to others. He often said, "I just wish that people could realize that anything is possible if you try. . . . Dreams are made if people try. . . ." And so he fashioned and followed his dream, a dream that would transform not only his own life but that of others.

—Through his suffering, Terry, who had not known God, discovered the importance in his life of a sense of God with him. When Terry's dream was again broken with the collapse in Thunder Bay he said, "If God is with me, then even if I die I win."

—Terry had persistence and determination. While he was fashioning his dream he said, "I'm a dreamer. I like challenges. I don't give up." He lived his own words so well that they captured the hearts and the lives of the people of Canada in such a way that when the run ended for Terry, the Marathon of Hope continued because others had caught his spirit.

In a "Tribute to Terry Fox," a reporter named Pat Kinsella said:

A man—alive
A life—lived
Not that it was short
But that it was full
He had a purpose.

Her words are reflective of Viktor Frankl's observation that when a person has a "why" to live, he can deal with any "how."

Pat Kinsella raises an important question in her tribute to Terry when she asks, "If he had not had cancer, would he have accomplished so much?" There is, of course, no answer. The question is a reminder to us of the place of suffering in human life. It is a challenge to us to find the meaning that is present in broken dreams rather than asking why we must suffer.

Finding hope in broken dreams

One of the most certain realities about broken dreams is that they are not places of life for everyone. We have all observed with sadness that not every tree that is cut down comes to some place of new life. We know that not every root seeks and responds to the scent of water which can lead to new life. Yet the words of Job and the following words of Joel remain true:

In the days to come—it is the Lord who speaks—
I will pour out my spirit on all mankind.

> Their sons and daughters shall prophesy,
> your young men shall see visions,
> your old men shall dream dreams.
>
> Acts 2:17

It is God's promise of a spirit present for all, a spirit poured out for all, a spirit out of which visions and dreams enough for life for all can emerge. How is it that this happens for some and not for others?

Essential to the vision and to the dream are the four keys of which we spoke earlier and then again through the lives of Max Cleland, of Lillian, and, most especially, of Terry Fox. But neither these keys nor their importance are self-evident. It is only through attentiveness to our own lives and through developing a habit of noticing the meaning in the lives of others can God's call to life receive from us the response that will bring meaning to unfolding dreams and the courage to let go of broken dreams.

If we think that it is only a matter of accepting the broken dream, we have not yet pursued the message to its final meaning. To have come to a place where we can cherish our broken dream not for itself but for the new life that emerged from it—it is to this that we are called by a God who loves us, and by our friend and companion, Jesus, whose dream for us is "life to the full."

1. *Letters to a Young Poet*, Rainer Maria Rilke (New York: Norton and Company, 1934).

IV
Noticing life

Because you are God's chosen ones, holy and beloved, clothe yourselves with heartfelt mercy, with kindness, humility, meekness and patience. Bear with one another; forgive whatever grievances you have against one another. Forgive as the Lord has forgiven you. Over all these virtues put on love, which binds the rest together and makes them perfect. Christ's peace must reign in your hearts, since as members of one body you have been called to that peace. Dedicate yourselves to thankfulness.

Colossians 3:12-15 (NAB)

Life continually brings good gifts to us, more gifts than we can accept and acknowledge, more than we can treasure with thankful hearts. One of life's tragedies is that we miss many of life's best gifts because we have not trained ourselves to notice them or, noticing them, we fear what accepting them will ask of us.

All too often we are like Estragon and Vladimir in Samuel Beckett's play *Waiting for Godot*. Like these two gentlemen of the road we claim to be waiting for the coming of a special person. But while we wait, we fail to notice all of the special people who are offering life to us. For us, and for Estragon and Vladimir, Godot never comes because we fail to make ourselves sensitive to how he will come and to what his presence will mean.

People complain of being lonely because special people or a special person is not there when needed. We live lonely because, while we wait for that person who will meet all our needs and fill our lonely spaces, we do not look around and notice the life that is already there for us. We are unable to receive the friendship that is offered because we put people in boxes, deciding that someone is too old or too young, too rich or too poor, too educated or too uneducated, male or female, black or white, of our culture or of a different one. Our preconceived notions of how that person who can be present to us should look or speak prevent us from seeing or hearing the presence of the person who is there. We would live richer lives if we were thankful for the life that comes to us in whatever form or person. Pozzo's words to Estragon and Vladimir are important for us:

> I too would be happy to meet him. The more people I meet the happier I become. From the meanest creature one departs wiser, richer, more conscious of one's blessings. Even you . . . even you, who knows, will have added to my store.[1]

I once had a long discussion with a friend who told me that I had been more fortunate than she because, when I needed them, people who cared for and supported me were always there. She doubted that there was even a single feeling of loneliness in my life.

Her sense of her own life was that she had not been so blessed, and that often no one was there for her. Her words reminded me of people who complain that they cannot see after they have chosen to put on some form of blinder, because she admitted that she had not taken some of the risks in relationships that had been a part of my life. Her words were a reminder of how different my life has been.

During the past five years of almost continual travel back and forth across this continent, I have spent many hours in airports, in conference centers, and in the presence of people with whom I have not had an opportunity to share life. Perhaps it is the survivor in me more than the prayerful and generous person who recognized that, unless I wished to be consumed by many lonely hours, I needed to cultivate an awareness of the life around me. I realized that before I could dedicate myself to thankfulness, I had to notice life and be open to it—through whatever channel it might come to me. I somehow knew that if I decided that only certain people, only the Godots of the world, would bring life to me, I would be rejecting some important gifts. I also might not have the daily nourishment that can come only from the presence of others.

We all need the presence of those who have walked a long part of the journey with us. These are the friends who give continuity to our lives, who are, for us, "roots."

Perhaps the central relationships of our lives, however, are eroded by our expectation that they will bring us all of life. I believe Pozzo is right when he says that every person we meet has something to say to our lives, that every person's gift matters. Our relationships are enriched by chance meetings, and by passing acquaintances who share with us, or with whom we can share.

I have flown on the same flights with the Denver Nuggets and the Milwaukee Bucks. I have flown with punk rock groups and members of symphony orchestras, with senior citizens and young children, with happy people and with those mourning as they were going home to the funeral of a loved one.

I once stayed in the same Houston hotel as the Philadelphia Phillies during the play-off games, and in a New York hotel with the Peking Ballet. I have cultivated a special interest in the street people of whatever city. In all of these and other experiences, I have found that my life was touched by the presence of these groups and by the conversations we shared. The presence of strangers with whom I shared life in whatever way has been important for me as I struggle with a deep strain of loneliness. It is a loneliness I no longer wish to remove, but with which I must deal, in which I want to find meaning and life.

Rhonda, the little balloon lady

I was flying from a religious education congress in
Spokane to Minneapolis. When I got on the plane, sitting in
the front row of the nonsmoking section and crying very
hard was a little girl. Kneeling beside her, and clearly not flying with her, was a young man. With tears streaming down
his face, he hugged the little girl as the cabin attendant announced that all visitors had to leave the plane. I have seen
this in so many airports in the country; "child visitation"
they call it.

I was sitting in the row behind the little girl, and I
reached to touch her shoulder and ask her if she wanted to
come and sit with me. As she turned her tear-stained face upward, she was crying too hard to speak and could only shake
her head to say "yes."

As I took her by the hand I asked her if she wanted to sit
in the center seat or by the window. She was very clear about
wanting to be near the window. As the plane was being
pushed back from the jetway, she was crying ever so quietly,
looking at the gate area in the airport and saying, in a barely
audible voice, "I want my daddy, I want my daddy." As she
spoke these words, her left hand was cupped around her face.
She was barely moving the fingers on her right hand as she
waved good-bye to her daddy.

This little child was bearing her pain with such dignity.
She was so protective of her daddy and told me later that she
had tried hard not to cry because she knew it was difficult for
him to leave her.

During the first hour of the flight my little friend told me
that she was almost five and that her name was Rhonda. She
reviewed, through her stories, all of the ways in which the
divorce experience affects children. She spoke of *her* divorce,
never of her *parents'* divorce; she believed that the divorce

was her fault because she had been naughty; she knew that both her daddy and mommy were hurting and so she didn't want them to know how she felt. She also believed that, if she was good, the divorce might not happen. Such large problems for one so small. Such inner burdens for which there was no present relief for her.

Then she turned to me, asked to borrow a Kleenex and dried her tears, as if to suggest that she wanted to think about something else now. She asked me if I wanted to see the presents her daddy and her grandfather had given her. She showed me a set of felt-tip markers and a coloring book that had some blank pages for "Rhonda originals." I asked her if she would make a picture for me. She asked me not to look so that the picture would be a surprise. When it was completed, she presented a picture of a lovely clown. When I asked her how she knew I had a special fondness for clowns, she looked so pleased. Then she put out her hand to take the picture again for a moment while telling me that she wanted to give her clown some balloons. When she handed the carefully drawn picture back to me with the balloons added, every balloon was black.

How I envied this little girl whose feelings were so clear to her. How grateful I felt for her trust in sharing them with me. What a paradox that picture was—the happy clown figure with the black balloons. How much it was like her life with its sadness of separation from her father and the periodic happy space of a visit with him and her grandfather.

As I was tucking the picture into my briefcase, the cabin attendant came to take Rhonda's bag to the front of the plane. Rhonda looked up, pointed a finger at her and said, "I don't want you to take my bag. This lady will do it," pointing to me. How quickly bonds form between people who share life.

When it was nearly time for us to land in Minneapolis, Rhonda tugged on my sleeve and said to me, "I'd like my picture back, please." With sadness and reluctance I reached for it and as I did she must have noticed my disappointment so she quickly consoled me by saying, "I want to make another for you." The second clown was nearly identical with the first but this time only two of the balloons were black. Somehow I believed it was her way of telling me that I had made her life a bit brighter that day.

As we were leaving the plane, she had to wait for a cabin attendant to take her and I had another flight for which I was nearly a half-hour late. She put her arms around me and kissed me and said, "You are a very nice lady. Thank you. Why were you so good to me?" I hugged her and said, "You are nice, too. I like you very much, Rhonda."

We said good-bye and parted. As I walked to my concourse my mind and my heart were filled with this child who had been such a gift to me. I felt so good about myself because, for me, it is very special to be loved by children. I spent the entire flight to Boston thinking about the qualities that I loved and had come to admire in this young child, qualities that she had been neither embarrassed nor afraid to share.

Rhonda was very much in touch with her feelings and she was trusting enough to share them, even with a stranger. I wish that at any given moment I could be that clear about how I feel and wise enough to entrust it to someone who would either help me accept the black balloons or help me exchange them, one by one, for a brightly colored balloon bouquet.

She was very good at making decisions and clear about what she wanted, whether it was where she would sit, who would carry her bag, or what she wanted to share with her father as he left her on the plane. I wondered why I so often have difficulty in making decisions or, even more often, why I sometimes hesitate to tell someone what I have decided.

Rhonda did not feel sorry for herself. She spoke much more of her daddy's pain than of her own. She was so sensitive to my short-lived disappointment of losing the clown that she quickly offered to make another. She who was so tiny and carried such large hurts made me realize my own ability to magnify small hurts and to let them fill all of the space inside of me. This quality reminded me of a song title, "I Haven't Got Time for the Pain," and of a poem entitled, "Even My Pain's Gonna Be Pretty."

Like Pozzo, Rhonda somehow knew that meeting people and sharing life with them was one sure way to become happier, one sure way to see another facet of life.

Because Rhonda liked herself she was not afraid to give others the opportunity to love her. She needed some reassurance from me that I cared as I left her, but through the hours that we shared, it was clear that she liked herself enough to believe that I cared.

By the time I reached Boston I had noted, in a journal that I keep, 27 qualities about Rhonda that I loved and admired. I did this because she had reached deep into my life, and thinking of her was a way of reliving the happy time we had shared. I did it as a reminder to myself to notice my own life a bit more and to see if I am doing as well as she did.

I do not know her last name, neither do I have an address or a phone number. If I ever see her again, she will be several inches taller and I will not recognize her. None of this matters. What does matter is that Rhonda was not a "waiting for Godot" kind of person and she gave me many reasons why I don't want to be one either.

I am thankful that I met Rhonda. My "dedication to

thankfulness" demands that I remain faithful to all that I learned from her about allowing others to be present by letting them into my life.

Kevin, my rescuer

The conference at Notre Dame was over and I left South Bend to fly home to Boston. I was weary from a long summer and dreaded even the brief layover in Detroit and the change of planes there.

I hurried from the plane to the departure gate in Detroit only to discover, much to my dismay, that the gate area was heavily populated with the wearers of white political candidates' hats because a national convention had ended that day. Realizing that this was not a day for me to get involved in a discussion of the platform of a political party, I was carefully calculating how I might avoid sitting next to one of these people. I decided to let the ticket agent take care of me, only to find that there was open-seating on that plane.

As I studied the situation I came up with three alternatives: put something on the seat next to me and, by my attitude, discourage anyone from sitting beside me; get on at some midpoint and hope for the best, or get on last and leave it to God.

Having had nearly an entire summer with a God who was close to the tough end of my concept of God as "tough and tender lover," I decided not to leave it to God and waited until about half of the gate area was empty.

When I got on the plane there was one unoccupied aisle seat near the front. Sitting in the adjacent seat, next to the window, was a little boy who I later learned was nine. You can imagine my delight when he informed me that the seat was not taken. I felt liberated from a situation that was not apt for me that day. Besides, as I began to think about it, it would be refreshing to get inside the world of that little boy during the two and a half-hour flight.

Fearing that I might frighten him if I seemed too interested, I was reviewing how I might initiate a conversation. He saved me any further effort when he tugged on my sleeve just as we were airborne and asked me the time. Not knowing how to keep the conversation going, I began again to think of some point of entry into his world. Soon, he tugged on my sleeve again and asked if I lived in Boston and, after my initial inner embarrassment, the conversation stopped only when he took from his pocket a long chunk of bubble gum. He broke off a piece for himself and was ready to put it back into his pocket when I could feel him looking at me out of the corner of his eye. He unwrapped the gum, broke off a second piece and said, "Hey, lady, can I share my bubble gum with you?"

As we shared the ritual of the bubble gum, we also shared some of what the summer had meant for each of us. I found him to be very interested in me and concerned in a surprisingly sensitive way about the fact that I had not yet taken a vacation.

There was a feeling of disappointment that the conversation was over when we landed at Logan. Not once since the beginning of the flight had I even remembered all those white hats around us.

When we were in the luggage claim area, we found one another again. A friend who met me at the airport had brought roses to welcome me home after six weeks away. I took one rose and walked over to give it to Kevin, my young friend. He received it with a smile and said, "Thanks, lady" and quickly left. I think he was afraid that I would kiss him and I surely would have.

His mother had been watching all of this and she said,

"May I ask how you and Kevin became friends?" When I told her what a wonderful son she had, she looked at me with the kind of disbelief parents sometimes have at how well their children manifest their best manners in public. She said, "I can't believe it. He never acts that way at home." But, even as she said it, there was also a kind of proud parent look on her face.

I never fly through Detroit without thinking of the day Kevin "rescued me" from the white political hats and from a weariness that disappeared by the time I got home.

I came to understand that sharing bubble gum is not something to take lightly. Kevin had scrutinized me carefully out of the corner of his eye. His own ability to take the initiative in conversation had prepared us well for that prized moment.

I realize that I would sometimes be less lonely if I were better at what was an art for him, a seemingly effortless art. He was not "waiting for Godot" before every conversation.

Garry Maddox, my only baseball hero

What I did not know when I left Boston for a Houston conference was that the Philadelphia Phillies, there for the play-offs, would be staying at the same hotel I was.

On the morning of my talk, I was pacing the hotel lobby and corridor in my usual nervous-before-a-talk way. I noticed a young boy with a bubble gum card in his hand approach a man for an autograph. As the man signed the card, a camera flash popped, as the boy's parents took a picture of him with his hero.

My perplexity at that moment was that I did not know who the player was and so I followed the little boy down the hall and asked him, "Who was that?" After his initial response of pity, his mood switched to an obvious disdain for anyone who would not have known who Garry Maddox was.

I returned to the lobby and, by that time, Garry Maddox was sitting by himself at one end of the lobby. I walked to where he was and asked if I might talk with him, asking him how it felt to be a major-league ballplayer on the day of so important a game. I was curious because of my own nervous and tense feelings before every talk I give.

He invited me to sit down and, after a brief moment of reflection, he shared with me some of the different ways players are affected by pre-game feelings. One thing he said has come to mind often, "You have to learn to make the tension work for you. People who can't do this are hurt by that inability. Perhaps this is one of the differences between a player and a great player. I believe that success is a matter of learning to manage anxiety and tension. You have to make it work for you instead of against you."

When I recall his words, I also recall the manner in which he spoke and the quiet reflectiveness in him. There was a gentle thoughtfulness about him, even in his willingness to spend a few minutes with a stranger.

When I told this story to a friend who follows baseball, he asked me if I had any idea of the kind of personal discipline required of a player like Garry Maddox; if I realized the demands on him to make it his business to study every batter and pitcher in the major leagues. I have thought about that often, for I have great personal regard for people who take their lives seriously and who enter into whatever they are doing out of faithfulness to their personal commitment to the life they have chosen.

I do not expect to see Garry Maddox again, but my life is richer because of that brief meeting and, when I think about him, I am thankful that I had the courage to ask the little boy who his hero was. I would have missed a meeting that gave me some new perspectives from which to view life.

The life of Jesus and our own

Not every person we meet will walk the whole journey with us. Not every person we meet will share with us in the same way and to the same extent. Shall we, therefore, choose not to meet them at all?

Martin Buber claims that "All real living is meeting." Though meeting is but the first step, it is the step that must be taken before others can follow. To refuse to be open to those first steps is to condemn ourselves to a loneliness from which there is no release and in which no life is to be found.

Our best model in this, as in all of human life, is Jesus. The gospels are rich with the open-ended stories of people with whom Jesus has intense meetings, meetings that call that person to relationship and to response. For most of these stories there is no immediate conclusion. The Samaritan woman at Jacob's well; Zacchaeus; the leper who returned to thank; Bartimaeus, the blind beggar; the woman with the hemorrhage; all have one thing in common. They approached Jesus out of some need in their own lives, approached him with no apparent desire for more than a momentary experience of this man Jesus. Each left him with a sense that much more had happened because Jesus is an involving lover, a persistent presence who does not easily go away.

The story of the life of each of these and many others was dramatically changed once they had let him into their lives at all. For them and for us, it is God's way of calling us to life. It is God's way of pursuing us until we notice and acknowledge a presence that is life for us. It is a presence that is God but a presence that can best be discovered in the faces of those we meet along the way.

The example of Jesus reminds us that there is a transforming power in human lives shared with openness and with sensitivity. As St. Paul says, because we are God's chosen ones, we must clothe ourselves with those human qualities that we give and receive in meeting and in sharing life. The gifts of Rhonda and Kevin and Garry are not less a part of my life than the gifts of friends whose presence has asked more of me. Their gifts enrich the ongoing relationships that need sustaining and are, therefore, more costly. I will not know how to take the large steps in approaching human intimacy if I fail to make the small ones. I will not have the courage to risk all if I am afraid to risk even a little. I will not experience that great sense of thankfulness in my life if I refuse the gifts that God continually offers through the presence of others. Pozzo's words are reflected again by Morris West:

> We were set to walk on separate paths. We've met most pleasantly at the crossroads. We'll part, each a little richer.[2]

1. *Waiting for Godot,* Samuel Beckett (New York: Grove Press, 1954).
2. *The Clowns of God,* Morris West (New York: William Morrow, 1981).

V
Acquiring a soul that is not flat, a soul that is not unused

Now on his return, having received his appointment as king, he sent for those servants to whom he had given the money, to find out what profit each had made. The first came in and said, "Sir, your one pound has brought in ten." "Well done, my good servant!" he replied. "Since you have proved yourself faithful in a very small thing, you shall have the government of ten cities." Then came the second and said, "Sir, your one pound has made five." To this one he said, "You shall be in charge of five cities." Next came the other and said, "Sir, here is your pound. I put it away safely in a piece of linen because I was afraid. . . ."

Luke 19:15-21

My inward journey in the companionship of loneliness has been a part of my life because I have found sustaining strength in the stories of the lives of others. From the pages of the Hebrew scriptures which tell the tales of the prophets and kings, through the gospels which reveal the life of Jesus and his followers, to stories told today in poetry, film, art, music and literature, I have discovered a common companion in my life and in the lives of others. This discovery has helped me to recognize loneliness as a life-giving companion because the lives of others reveal that this was so for them. Stories of their life journeys, made in the companionship of loneliness, reveal what a prodding and soul-stretching presence it is. A companion we would never seek, loneliness is yet, in retrospect, a cherished presence. It is a talent with which life invites us to trade.

My sense of the goodness, the richness and the strength

that can be found in stories is a gift I received from a friend, a man whose place in my life begins with me.

My earliest memories of him are of me sitting on his lap, listening to his stories. My most cherished gift, even today, a book, is a reminder of my happiness when this friend brought me storybooks, books I could only hug when I was too young to read.

Recalling what I can about his stories brings back both the qualities of the stories and of the man. Remembering both his stories and him gives me some insights into his life that I am sure I did not have as a child. Remembering the stories and the man is important because the stories I read now and the qualities I look for in friends are somehow related to him whose love for me challenges me to write my own story with care and love. His love challenges me to enter into the loneliness that is a part of my story as it was a part of his.

In the security of his arms, I listened to stories that were always open-ended and always about doing good for others. Whether it was a big black bear, a little girl or an Olympic runner, the principal figure was involved in doing something good for someone else and often at the risk of losing something very important.

Sometimes the same stories were repeated over and over with only the change of one small part which, of course, changed the ending. I could never persuade this storyteller to give me any hints about the ending. The fun of stories, he told me, was that you did not know the end at the beginning. But he also taught me that, if I noticed what the people in his stories were doing and how they were treating other people, I could get some hint of the ending. Sometimes he even stopped to ask me to tell him what I thought the ending would be.

When I was older, and still liked to sit on his lap and

listen to his stories, he told me that in real life people are writing the end of their own stories at the beginning and all along the way.

It is a curious thing that even though this man never told me stories about Jesus or other people in the Bible, or stories about God—for he was not a pious man as people often mistakenly think of piety—my understanding of God's stories makes sense to me today because this man taught me how to listen to stories. He taught me what to notice in them as they unfolded so that I might enjoy each story more.

So well were those stories told in my childhood that I see a relationship between them and the stories that are life-sustaining for me now. His gift was that he expanded, through his stories, not only my vision of life but even my heart and soul. It was a gift for me that he was not afraid to share his own story with me and to tell me about its lonely places.

A soul that is not flat, a heart that is not narrow

One of the challenges that we continually face is to find meaning in the ordinary and to find new insights in old truths. The people who have helped me to do this are primarily those who tell stories, whether in dance or song, in pictures or in words. It is the uncommon gift of the artist as storyteller to lead us into some new or more meaningful way of perceiving that at which we often look. We are not invited, necessarily, to look at new things so much as we are called to see the things at which we look, to see them with our hearts as well as with our eyes. We are invited by good storytellers to the biblical way of hearing and seeing which involves being present to that which we hear and see. The artist encourages us to look and then look again, with the confidence that we will see something the second time that first evaded our notice.

The storyteller, through whatever medium, continually recreates the ability to see more life in the very process of risking the vision through the art of sharing it with another. The storyteller continually trades a personal talent in an unforeseen way because telling our story opens us to the stories of others.

Through the willingness of the storyteller to tell her own story, she becomes a direction finder for us, revealing our lives to us before they happen so that, when they do, we will understand them better. In the very act of risking and trading talents, the artist discovers new ways of seeing and hearing and then shares them with us again and again. Through the artist's effort to frame human experience in some form of story, she shares not only her own story but yours and mine. The artist as storyteller, in the act of articulating a story she knows or wishes to know better, frees me to see my own story more clearly and leads me to want to share what I see.

My memories of my favorite storyteller, though always present to me, were reviewed and renewed at the time of my last annual retreat. It is my usual practice to go to retreat with only two books, my Jerusalem Bible and one book of poetry. Each year I explore the collected works of some poet. This year that poetry book, the gift of some of my sisters for whom I had directed a retreat, was *Collected Poems* by Edna St. Vincent Millay. Being unfamiliar with most of her poems and having lost my childhood penchant to want to know the end at the beginning, in story if not in real life, I began with the first poem. I also ended there because I never got beyond the first poem, one she called "Renascence." Its riches led me on a retreat-long journey which continues now. In its essence the poem reminded me so much of my storytelling friend that it was like a journey made with him, an invitation to remember the lessons of his stories and his life. Through the beauty of Millay's words I rediscovered the messages he gave to me as much by his life as through his words.

Through the telling of a story that was only 11 pages long, Edna St. Vincent Millay took me on a condensed but powerfully moving journey through some chapters of my own life. I identified with her frustration in feeling so hemmed in by three mountains and a wood, over which she could not see. This frustration led her to notice the one thing that seemed not to make her world small, but rather freed her to see and reach as far as she could. So she stretched out on the grass in an effort to reach and touch the sky.

As she did this, the boundaries of her life fell away making the poem a journey through the seasons, to faraway places, and to people both in love and in need. In the telling, she was opened again to the places of suffering and of intense happiness not easy to contain in words, yet identified so well by her as to seem like my own. How grateful I am that she was willing to share her gift, one which, if hoarded or buried, would have made life a little less for both of us.

In the final words of her poem she sketches for me a portrait of my storytelling friends, all of them, each of them. She calls each of us to embrace the loneliness of risking and sharing in the name of whom we can become when we do.

> The world stands out on either side
> No wider than the chart is wide;
> Above the world is stretched the sky—
> No higher than the soul is high.
> The heart can push the sea and land
> Farther away on either hand;
> The soul can split the sky in two,
> And let the face of God shine through.
> But East and West will pinch the heart
> That can not keep them pushed apart;
> And he whose soul is flat—the sky
> Will cave in on him by and by.[1]

I can envision no more lonely place of life than having a "flat soul" and a "narrow heart." It is a part of the paradox of life I also believe that the only way to claim a soul that is "high" and a heart that is "wide" is through entering into the inner loneliness that we all know while at the same time owning the risks that cannot be avoided along the way. Closing doors to new possibilities, building walls that I think will keep me safe from hurt, remaining silent whether with friends or enemies, avoiding having my vision of life rejected, refusing to share my story in whatever way—is to choose, even without conscious awareness, a flat soul and a narrow heart. It is to betray the storytellers who have traded their talents and invested them in my life to make my world larger. For me to do that would be to forget one of God's best gifts in my life, the early and faithful presence of a gifted storyteller. It would be to forget the gifts of this man, gifts which remain with me today as I remember his power and goodness. His are the same gifts that I perceive in others whose stories, told in whatever medium, have given me the courage to trade and invest my own talents rather than follow the security-seeking way of the servant who "put the talent away safely in a piece of linen."

The gifts of one whose soul was not flat,
whose heart was not narrow

A love for the beauty of the earth and an ability to communicate that love. I have never had a close friend who did not notice, seek to share and want to speak about the beauty of the earth. I have lived all of my life in places where there were four distinct seasons, and sharing those seasons with friends is one of my most cherished experiences. The best release I find from any form of inner tension is in the enjoyment of the beauty of whatever season and in whatever place I am. The poetry, art and literature in which I discover the deepest meaning in some way expresses one of God's greatest gifts, that of the goodness and beauty of life as it is reflected in the world of nature.

A desire to share the gifts that one has. The nature of the life reflected in the beauty of the earth and in those people whose lives intersect with ours brings with it the reminder that no gift is given to us for ourselves alone. A gift received is a gift to be shared; it has no other reason for being a part of our lives. Like the story of the servants, a gift given away comes back to us in renewed life; a gift hidden is eventually lost, even to ourselves. When my storytelling friend died, a card found in one of his books, a card describing him very accurately, helped me understand where the power in his stories had come from. It read:

> I shall pass this way but once.
> Any good thing that I can do, therefore,
> Or any kindness that I can show
> To any other human being,
> Let me do it now.
> Let me not defer it or neglect it.
> For, I shall not pass this way again.
>> (An epitaph found on an obscure
>> gravestone in an old cemetery in England)

Sharing the gifts one has in an unassuming manner, in a manner respectful of the gifts of every other person. Through all of my life the people who have left the deepest impression on me are those who were not overly impressed with themselves. It is a delightful experience to meet people of great and publicly acclaimed talent and to leave them having been welcomed into their presence with such graciousness that we feel our presence gave them some gift which they recognized. If I were to measure the difference between the truly great and the would-be great, it would have to be related to this quality.

It is a quality that reflects one of the meanings of the words of Matthew:

> Be careful not to parade your good deeds before men to attract their notice; by doing this you will lose all reward from your Father in heaven. So when you give alms, do not have it trumpeted before you; this is what the hypocrites do in the synagogues and in the streets to win men's admiration. I tell you solemnly, they have had their reward. But when you give alms, your left hand must not know what your right hand is doing.
>
> Matthew 6:1-3

Perhaps what the words of the gospel writer suggest to us is that "parading our good deeds" may be related to missing the meaning of our lives by continually wishing to see them for more than they are, while missing the goodness and beauty in exactly what they are. The reward of life, which the artist helps us to discover, is in seeking continually to discover the gifts always present in us and so to be more respectful of the gifts present in others.

Risking what we have for the sake of what we can become. One of the greatest obstacles to life is our refusal to let go of what we have in order to grow to some new place. However little we have, we cling to it with some sense of security, even sometimes when we have identified it as a place of destruction.

The story is told of an artist who lived and worked on an obscure island. His most prized possession was a metal sculpture which he had fashioned through several years. In the process of molding and remolding it he recognized that, as an artist and as a man, he had grown with his own work. In his fondness for the work of his own hands he had the growing realization that this very work had even led him to grow beyond what he had expressed through it. So he went in search of metal out of which to form another sculpture, one that would be of even greater beauty.

With disappointment he learned that there was no more metal on that tiny island. If he wished to produce another work of art, a work that would express his own growth, he could only do it by melting and remolding his first master-piece.

One can give either of two endings to the tale. The end-ing we choose and the reasons why, will reveal as much about ourselves as about the artist and his dilemma.

Beginnings and endings are a part of life. They are times of loneliness. How we do the first has much to do with deter-mining how we will do the second. Whether or not we choose to do either well is set in this reality—we cannot grow to some new place of life if we are unwilling to leave the place we are now.

Becoming a person who is faithful to prayer. Prayer takes many forms: saying words, listening, noticing life, searching for meaning, being present to a God who is always present to us, asking questions about the direction of life. These and many other ways of praying, to which we are faithfully committed, are the means by which any person is slowly transformed into a prayerful person. Without a per-sonal belief in the value of self-reflection we do not become self-reflective people—people who are able to set in perspec-tive the relationship between past, present and future. This sense of our own personal history enables us to stand in the present and live there because we value the heritage of our own past so as to give shape and direction to the future.

Becoming a prayerful person whose life has direction grows out of my attentiveness to my own story, and my ef-forts to understand it by reflecting on the meaning of the story of Jesus. Prayer leads me to believe in the value of my story through telling it to God, as I understand it, and then listening to God as his story for me unfolds in my life.

The artists who have shared their story with me have

taught me how to pray. Something about the qualities of their lives as expressed in their work expands my vision of life and continually calls me to go back to the challenge of the soul that is not flat and the heart that is not narrow.

The persistent presence of my storytelling friend

I never realized how blessed I was to have grown up with an excitement about the goodness and the value of stories. As a child it never occurred to me that there were children who felt lonely because they did not have the gift of a parent or a friend to lead them into their own world by walking with them into worlds not their own.

I did not realize then, and I wish I did not know it to be true now, that there are children who never had a friend from whose secure arms they could look unafraid at what is larger than or less than life, or see life for what it is and what it can become.

It is only now, in thinking back on the stories my friend told me, that I discover their meaning in ways I could not understand then. How does a child comprehend an adult's sense of satisfaction in life, satisfaction told in countless ways through stories, satisfaction rooted in the conviction that life matters and makes sense when we seek to give to others every gift given to us? Even an adult might not understand a man who believes that his life will be worthwhile if only one person is better because he is willing to share what he has.

A child does not easily understand a friend who believes that he ought never decide to close a door until he has looked to see what is on the other side. Even a story about Peter Rabbit or Paul Bunyan could set that same child thinking about it. And the presence of such a man would be assurance that he would not be punished by living with regrets of unexplored life or of good deeds undone. Though I did not realize it at the time, my storyteller's message of the gospel was as clear and as profound as that of Matthew, Mark, Luke or John.

His convictions about the possibilities of life and our responsibility to both explore and share them remind me of the words of Bernanos in *The Diary of a Country Priest:*

> Won't damnation be the tardy discovery, the discovery much too late, after death, of a soul absolutely unused, still carefully folded together, and spoiled, the way precious silks are spoiled when they are not used?[2]

How many people have kept their souls "folded up" and tucked away, fearing the loneliness of rejection or misunderstanding?

My storytelling friend helped me to look up at the sky, and in his own way, to try to reach it. His was no small heart, no heart that refused to give or receive love. His was not a heart afraid of life. And sometimes, when I sensed a sadness in my friend, I wondered who might have refused to share with him the life he offered. Was he lonely then?

I have no tangible way to ask him these questions, for he died many years ago. And though I still talk with him and tell him my own stories, I am never quite sure how time has changed my perceptions of him. Do I see who he was then out of who I am now, rather than reaching to discover who he is now while I continue to discover who I am?

This storytelling friend taught me much about life, this man whose arms gave me both inner freedom and security, as I listened to his stories.

His were arms that set me free, even as a child. They were arms that held me tight and gave me the sense of being loved unconditionally. The securest place in the world for me as a child was in his arms. To be told another story was one of my life's greatest gifts.

Because he taught me how it feels to be held by arms that are freeing, he calls me to a kind of accountability when my own arms are not freeing for others. And he calls me to an awareness of when the arms of others are not freeing for me.

I love this man. I remember him well. I still feel secure in his love. He was one of God's best gifts to my life. He is my father, the man I called "my daddy."

1. *Collected Poems*, Edna St. Vincent Millay (New York: Harper & Row, paperback edition).
2. *The Diary of a Country Priest*, Georges Bernanos (New York: Macmillan, 1962).

VI
Saying yes to life

Do you really think that when I am making my plans, my motives are ordinary human ones and that I say Yes, yes and No, no, at the same time? I swear by God's truth, that there is no Yes and No about what we say to you. The Son of God, the Christ Jesus that we proclaimed among you . . . was never Yes and No; with him it was always Yes, and however many the promises God made, the Yes to them all is in him. That is why it is "through him" that we answer Amen to the praise of God.

2 Corinthians 1:18-20

The central experience of loneliness is not a matter of being with another or alone, or a question of having many friends or a few. It is not related to some inherent personality weakness. At the heart of loneliness is a question of personal integrity, of our ability and willingness to follow our own truth, regardless of the cost to us, after we have made the effort to discover it.

At the heart of loneliness is the choice we are called to make to follow our convictions and to respond to a call that never allows us to rest. At the heart of loneliness is our entrance into that inward journey, a journey we will begin and continue only if we have said yes to a life that is not yet, that one day can be.

To freely and consistently say yes to life is a way of life we choose through countless small and seemingly insignificant choices. It is not a single conversion experience; it is the result of many small and large conversion experiences. If we understood better what conversion means and when it takes place in us, we would understand more fully what it meant for Jesus to be a person who lived his yes to life. Repeating our yes as Jesus did, could become a posture toward life that we want to make our own.

It is a misfortune that conversion experiences of others have been portrayed as some instantaneous event that causes a person's entire life to be different. The classic example often invoked is Saul's immediate and nearly total transformation after he was unexpectedly struck to the ground on the way to Damascus. To view what happened in this manner is to forget the story of Saul's life, both before and after his famous journey. To look upon the change in Saul's life-direction is to ignore both the sincerity and intensity with which he lived what he believed to be faithful to Yahweh's plan for him. Conversions can never be sudden, though we may believe they are if we know the life of the individual only superficially.

To read Acts 9:1-20 and to speak of it as an experience of sudden conversion is to fail to listen to Saul's own words about that event. Saul did not experience a call to something completely new as much as it was a call to a deeper level of life in God. Saul never apologizes for who he was. He calls attention to the fact that just as he was a good pharisee, now he responds faithfully to the new direction he has received.

Saul, at whose feet the murderers of Stephen had laid down their cloaks, is called by God to be the one to welcome the gentiles to a vision of life far wider than Judaism.

Saul is an example to us not because of the suddenness of the experience but because of his faithfulness to what he had heard and seen through all of his life. He is an example of one whose relentless pursuit of life in response to Yahweh's call reminds us to continually reexamine the direction of our lives and to search for deeper meaning.

When Saul arose from the ground "even with his eyes wide open he could see nothing at all" (Acts 9:8), no doubt a fearsome place for one so active as he.

When I think of Saul who became Paul, I wonder how it was for him after Ananias, the unlikely prophet who welcomed him to the community, had left him—after Ananias had laid hands on him and the scales fell from his eyes.

Once Saul could see, he was called to go back and preach to the same people he had sought to put to death. No easy human call, it must have caused him some moments when he wondered, "What will people think and say?"

Experiences like Saul's, experiences of what we say is "sudden conversion," remind us that the yes to life we seek is like the faithful and gradual turning of plants toward the sun, or the tenacity of the tender shoot as it pushes its way through the soil. We grow to be faithful to life as Jesus was, only by accepting and coming to terms with the human ways by which we gradually discover where life is for us.

Our yes is a multifaceted word

While holding the consistency and faithfulness of Jesus as an ideal toward which to grow, we are daily confronted with our sometimes impulsive and sometimes fitful response. We find consolation in the gospel story of the two brothers:

> "What is your opinion? A man had two sons. He went and said to the first, 'My boy, you go and work in the vineyard today.' He answered, 'I will not go,' but afterwards thought better of it and went. The man then went and said the same thing to the second who answered, 'Certainly, sir,' but did not go. Which of the two did the father's will?"
>
> Matthew 21:28-31

We find hope in that story because sometimes we say no while searching for strength inside ourselves to do what we have just refused to do. We identify with the son who, having said no immediately set out to discover a way to do what his father had asked.

Sometimes we say no to a life question that demands a

yes because we are haunted with the memory of a past yes that was not possible for us, a yes that led to a failure or rejection. We say no not because we are cowards but because both our memories and our feelings plague us. Past failure and its present pain would lead us to a search for security where no is safer than the possibility of some new pain of another yes. We are continually confronted with each costly risk for life.

Sometimes we are at once a yes-and-no person somehow believing we will find life in a some-of-each existence. We fear to choose because we know what we have and are uncertain about what we might gain or lose. Dag Hammarskjold writes that if we are unable to accept the axiom that if we choose one path we will be denied the others, we must then try to persuade ourselves "that the logical thing to do is to remain at the crossroads."[1] We become like the people William Glasser speaks of when he says that there is in them something that prefers known misery to unknown happiness. We become people who trick ourselves into believing that avoiding mistakes is the goal of all of life. When we do this, we are not avoiding mistakes, we are avoiding life itself. What we do not trust is not life but ourselves.

Growing toward a yes stance will lead us through some days of maybe. What makes a difference is if we use the maybe days to deliberately set our lives in a holding pattern because we refuse to give serious thought to life itself, or if we use them to scrutinize life's possibilities, carefully evaluating when a yes is for life, or when it will destroy life.

Being open to life means saying yes to life, but that is not the same as saying yes to everything that enters our lives. Part of the growth toward our yes is to know the difference between what leads to maturity and what leads to a destruction of my sense of who I am. How can we discover this difference? There is no formula for unlocking the secret of maturity, only the continual invitation to try to do so because the growth toward it is growth toward life.

> A mature man is his own judge. When all is said and done, his one firm support is his loyalty to his own convictions. The counsel of others may be welcome and valuable, but it does not release him from responsibility; therefore, he may become very lonely.[2]

The story of the two brothers carries with it the haunting reminder that we, like each of them, grow daily more or less faithful to ourselves and to our lives through our choices. It reminds us of the difference between the response of the brother and the faithful yes of Jesus.

Our desire to become like Jesus, our desire to be able to count on ourselves for faithfulness to God's call to life, our willingness to walk the same lonely way as Jesus—all are inspired and nourished by the lives of others whose example tells us of their faithfulness to their own yes to life.

Dag Hammarskjold:
The acclaimed public servant and the inner lonely person

Great men and women of every age have given the priceless gift of believing that a single, well-lived life leaves its mark even on a society as complex as our own. And somehow we feel personally betrayed by public figures for whom personal integrity was less important than some other value they chose.

When a public servant has lived according to the inner dictates of a faithfully formed conscience to such an extent that even the bitterest critics give public testimony to that fact, every person shares in that person's gift to the world.

The whole world mourned the death of one such servant, former United Nations Secretary General Dag Hammarskjold. We have some insights into his life in the words of a young woman at the UN when she said of Hammarskjold on his death, "Why did so many weep? Because he was the best in all of us . . . the generous in each of us. . . ."

Though Dag Hammarskjold once said that there was no formula for teaching another how to arrive at maturity and no words adequate to express the language of the inner life, he was a man whose life formula emerged from and took form in a single word:

> I don't know Who—or what—put the question, I don't
> know when it was put. I don't even remember answering.
> But at some moment I did say yes to Someone—or
> Something—and from that hour I was certain that ex-
> istence is meaningful and that, therefore, my life, in self-
> surrender had a goal. . . . As I continued along the Way, I
> learned, step by step, that behind every saying in the
> Gospels stands one man and one man's experience.[3]

Hammarskjold's life was rooted in all that is basic to the message of the gospel and the meaning of the Christian tradi-tion of prayer. Examining those things which he tells us were for him the keys to choosing what was a continually costly yes to life can be helpful in identifying the keys for our lives.

Hammarskjold was widely acclaimed for his role as a public servant. It seems unusual that the qualities of the in-ner person were not even recognized by his closest associates until his spiritual legacy was revealed, after his death, in the publication of his book, *Markings*.

Out of his cherished mountain climbing experiences he recorded the "trail marks" of his journey which he regarded as his own personal negotiation with his God. He wrote them as personal reminders of where he had been on his journey, and in faithfulness to Soren Kierkegaard's principle that "we live our lives forward, but we understand them backwards."

We met this public servant through his television ap-pearances and on the pages of our daily papers. We recognized the quality of leadership he gave to the developing young organization that sought to build world community. Seldom has any servant of peace paid the ultimate price for a vision—one that led him to Africa where he was martyred by those who opposed it. *Markings* reveals his firm commitment to his values even though they led him to his death. What his public life gave witness to was a man of profound inner strength. But, for whatever reasons, until *Markings* was published in 1964, his faithful commitment to prayer in emulation of the Christian mystics whose works he had studied was not recognized.

The legacy of the "trail marks" of his inner journey, recorded as early as 1925, is his invitation to others to believe in and make a commitment to that same journey. "The longest journey we make," he wrote, "is the journey inward," acknowledging that the price of servanthood informed by prayer is immeasurable. In Hammarskjold the coming together of the best of human gifts and the most costly kind of grace made him the public servant whose life was sustained by the continuing prayer of the inner person.

When I first read *Markings* early in 1965 I was inspired by his description of the emergence of his own yes to life. His words reveal the uncertainty in which it began when he speaks of saying yes to a presence not clear to him. But as I followed, with great interest, the inner journey revealed through those dated markings, it was like having a window onto the emergence of a yes that could no longer act in opposition to itself. I treasured his inner journey and sought to imitate what I had learned from him.

It was only in 1978 when I was asked to give a presentation on the life of Dag Hammarskjold for a "Spiritual Biography Series" that I set about to find and read every biography of Hammarskjold that I could find. It is partly my own fascination with his story and partly my eagerness to identify with him in whatever aspects of my journey are like his, that keeps a marker in at least one of his biographies at all times.

For me, the pearl of great price in the journal of his soul is more than his identification with the yes of Jesus in his response to the demands of public life. It was his own revelation of the sometimes terrifying loneliness that was a companion through all his life. It is said of him that loneliness was his vocation.

If his yes revealed the best of public service, its underlying and recurrent theme was his loneliness. If his yes eventually became the larger than life tapestry best portraying who he was, it was the threads of loneliness that added the subtlety of color responsible for the beauty of that tapestry. If his yes was the framework for the brilliant speeches that challenged world leaders, the agony of reaching across a desolate sense of loneliness was its mysterious source. His yes was a way of life for him of which he said, "It is not we who seek the Way, but the Way which seeks us." Because of this, "For him who has responded to the call of the Way of Possibility, loneliness may be obligatory."[4]

The roots of the inner person

Biographers of Hammarskjold generally agree that three forces had molded his strong spirit: his family and his fatherland, his love of nature, and his faith. Each of these forces was like a gift for life that he had received. Each was a gift in faithfulness to which, like the faithful steward in the gospel, he had tended and traded and in relation to which he had grown.

Hammarskjold's father and his three brothers were involved in politics and were recognized as effective public servants in Sweden. They were servants known to be willing to pay a high personal price for serving with clear dedication. It was a service rooted in faith in God and a love for Sweden, a service so well recognized that when a job required the rare combination of sensitivity and ability, the word in Sweden was "Try one of the Hammarskjolds."

The public life of his father, whom Hammarskjold spoke of as a mature man, was linked with a mother whose role in the home was important because of his frequent absences. This was a combination suited to the continued growth of the Christian faith which had been at the heart of the life of the family.

When a man leaves such a home to pursue a career in public service, and when both his faith and his intense commitment to serve well are so deeply rooted, the meaning of family is revealed at its best.

Living in Sweden, it is not surprising that his love for nature grew out of and was nourished through his skill as a mountain climber. Even as Secretary General, returning to his homeland to scale his favorite peaks was a cherished opportunity to renew his sense of the importance of personal discipline and finely tuned powers of observation. He said that the qualities that climbing required of him were exactly those which he needed in public life: perseverance and patience, a firm grip on realities, careful and imaginative planning linked with an awareness of the dangers. His belief was clear that "the safest climber is he who never questions his ability to overcome all difficulties."

Hammarskjold was a man whose disciplined life of public service and whose dreams for the life of the inner person were so fused that one could not be separated from the other. His relentless demands on himself, his ongoing and restless fear that he was less than he desired to be, made him a human furnace in which the gold of his yes to life was continually being refined.

It was the third of his gifts, nourished and sustained by

the others, that gave the final direction to his life. The first to implant and foster this faith had been his father and mother, but he was a man wise enough to observe the truth in the lives of others and to relate that truth to his own life.

In his creed, once presented on radio by Edward R. Murrow, Hammarskjold attributed to the soldiers and government officials in his father's family, his belief that no life was more satisfying than one of selfless service to your country and humanity. He also believed that such service required a sacrifice of all personal interest.

In that same creed he revealed that his convictions about the way a man should live had been discovered in and nourished by the writings of the medieval mystics. For them "self-surrender had been the way to self-realization and . . . in 'singleness of mind' and 'inwardness' [they] had found the strength to say yes to every demand which the needs of their neighbors made them face, and to say yes to every fate life had in store for them. . . ."[5]

His faith was nourished by his interest in all forms of art and literature. It was a living faith able to see the connections between the best in one's own experience and that of others. It was a faith that was then able to see all of this as God's way of calling us to live more faithfully.

Even in the complicated structure of the United Nations he manifested his dedication to the value of each individual life, and lived by one of Albert Schweitzer's dicta: "I ought to treat all lives as if they were my own." He was familiar with the *Imitation of Christ* of Thomas à Kempis, and with the writings and the person of Martin Buber.

Nourishing his own demanding inner spirit deepened each of the three elements in his faith, elements which he himself identified in an order which eventually was reversed in his life: the intimate presence of the living God, the example of Jesus, and the imperative of duty.

Led first by that persistent element which was to emerge very early in his life, that element which was a non-negotiable conviction that he was obliged to a life of public service, he was drawn into greater personal reflection on the life of Jesus and its meaning. From there he was drawn to an abiding and powerful sense of the presence of God with him.

His life is living testimony to the truth that grace builds on and works through nature. How else would such a person approach his own journey to discover the inner person except in the political life to which he was called? What other way could there have been through which the meaning of the message of the mystics would take flesh in his life? How natural it was for him to say that, "In our era, the road to holiness passes necessarily through the world of action."

The markings of the man

Out of the recurring themes in his own life, themes on which he reflected in *Markings*, we discover that all of his life could be traced to a very few sacred values. They are values that could emerge only in a person whose life of prayer had given him a sense of an ever-present strength that was more than his own. It was a presence he recognized and named God. Only in relationship to this presence, and to the meaning he discovered, through personal prayer, in the life of Jesus, the public servant and the inner man came to be like Jesus in the faithfulness of his yes to life.

Self-sacrifice and generous service were so much a part of his life that Hammarskjold spoke of them only as one can who takes them for granted in himself and respects them in others. He seemed to turn so naturally to these values that we are left with no noticeable or clearly identifiable external conversion experiences. Unlike Saul, each response he offered to life was related to greater depth, though not to a difference of direction.

To look at the quality of his life and to fail to remember the personal price it asked of him misses the meaning of the imperceptible workings of grace in the heart and soul of a faithful Christian.

His acknowledgment of the gifts that other faithful lives brought into his own made him a man who heeded Paul's words in Colossians 3, "You are God's chosen race, his saints; he loves you. . . . Therefore, dedicate yourselves to thankfulness." His relationships with world leaders, and with those who staffed the United Nations in whatever positions, revealed a man whose dedication to life and gentle gratitude for others flowed out of a life that continually said, "For all that has been, thanks; to all that will be, yes."

But, of all the markings of this man, the one of which he most often spoke and the one from which he never sought escape was his inner goad of personal loneliness. It was in relationship to this companion that he most understood the meaning of sacrifice and discipline. For a man who was continually in the company of world leaders, for one whose life had a profound impact on the lives of both his friends and his enemies, it is difficult to imagine his pain in a statement so simple as, "I do not dare to believe, I do not see how I shall ever be able to believe, that I am not alone."[6]

For him, just as surely as the road to holiness necessarily passed through the world of action, so the way to saying and living his yes to life could only be made possible by entering into his own loneliness. Perhaps it is only in this way that we discover, as he did, what it means to give a selfless love, a love he spoke of in a poem about Christ, a poem that also reveals himself:

> The burden remained mine:
> They could not hear my call,
> And all was silence.

What will their love help there?
There, the question is only
If I love them . . .[7]

1. *Markings*, Dag Hammarskjold (New York: Alfred A. Knopf, 1964).
2. *Dag Hammarskjold: A Spiritual Portrait*, Sven StolpeCharles (New York: Charles Scribner's Sons, 1966).
3. *Markings*.
4. *Ibid*.
5. *Ibid*.
6. *Ibid*.
7. *Ibid*.

VII
Seeing—
all of life consists in this

Having this hope, we can be quite confident; not like Moses, who put a veil over his face so that the Israelites would not notice the ending of what had to fade. And anyway, their minds had been dulled; indeed, to this very day, that same veil is still there when the old covenant is being read, a veil never lifted, since Christ alone can remove it. Yes, even today, whenever Moses is read, the veil is over their minds. It will not be removed until they turn to the Lord. Now this Lord is the Spirit, and where the Spirit of the Lord is, there is freedom. And we, with our unveiled faces reflecting like mirrors the brightness of the Lord, all grow brighter and brighter until we are turned into the image that we reflect; this is the work of the Lord who is Spirit.

2 Corinthians 3:12-18

My life is revealed to me by what I see and choose to look at as well as by what I fail to see or refuse to look at. I sometimes fit the description of Saul in Acts when the writer says of him, "even with his eyes wide open, he could see nothing at all" (Acts 9:8). At other times I have seen far even when my life was shrouded in some form of inner darkness. I have experienced loneliness when I could not see clearly the direction that would lead to greater life. But I have also felt lonely and afraid when I saw exactly the response that life asked of me.

To speak of the gift of sight as if it were every person's gift is to forget or ignore the lives of many people whose view of life does not come through their eyes. To speak of the seeing that is related more to insight than to sight as if it were a way of life for all fails to acknowledge that all such grace is costly.

Jesus' invitation is not an easy one to follow faithfully and
without fear:
> "Walk while you have the light,
> or the dark will overtake you;
> he who walks in the dark does not know where he is
>   going.
> While you have the light,
> believe in the light
> and you will become the sons of light."
>
> John 12:35-36

His invitation reminds us that if we choose to ignore the
light or walk away from it, we may find ourselves immersed
in darkness without being aware of exactly how it came upon
us. And whether we choose to walk in light or in darkness,
we will be accompanied by loneliness.

Choosing to walk in light is not a single choice, nor is it a
simple commitment. It carries with it a call to faithfulness to
what I see, even when others do not see it, or see differently.
It demands a willingness to share my vision, otherwise the vision cannot grow. Providing for the growth of the life I see requires careful self-reflection. There is a price to be paid for
nourishing the vision and following it. It can sometimes involve the risk of loss of friends and companions who see differently or fear what I see. But there is also the hope and joy
that can come only through trusting the vision.

I have lived my life almost exclusively in a seeing world.
Sometimes reflecting on the world of the sightless has given
me valuable insights. The nonseeing world was opened to
me by a young woman named Jackie. The thing I remember
best about her is that she was one of the happiest people I
have ever met.

She was a student in a high school biology class I taught.
I remember my surprise when, in working with her lab part-
ner, she would describe what she was working with as though

she had used the microscope. She was a student leader, a member of the debate team, an accomplished musician, an excellent student and a marvelously independent person. She was also somewhat of an upsetting presence to her seeing classmates whose vision of life was not equal to hers.

Discussions with Jackie and with her parents revealed to me the careful help her parents had gotten for themselves so that they would not destroy the possibility of a rich and full life for a daughter blinded since birth. The choices Jackie and her parents made formed a young woman whose vision of life and whose goals for herself were more clear than those of most other students her age. She did not speak of loneliness in the same ways her classmates did. Hers was the loneliness of one forced by circumstances to walk a unique way.

Because of her hopefulness about life and her faithful commitment to the life she sought regardless of the personal cost to her, Jackie is a symbolic presence for me now. In a unique way she personifies the meaning of Jesus' invitation to walk in light so it becomes both a way of life and a way to life. Her life consisted in seeing.

My memory of Jackie has often led me to notice and listen carefully to the lives of others whose commitment to seeing was faithful and also costly. She is a reminder of how much I love and admire people who pay the price for the ability to see far, and who share what they see in a stance of vulnerability to those who differ. They do not shrink from the inevitable loneliness that will flow from such fidelity.

Jackie is a frightening reminder to me of the life that is lost both for individuals and nations because of their refusal either to see or to follow a vision. History carries the stories of visionaries whose gift was wrested from them by others more powerful who prevented them from sharing their vision. Someone observed that Christianity has often killed its prophets and then canonized its martyrs because a live visionary presents a challenge never offered in quite the same way by a dead martyr.

Where does accountability lie for lost visions? Is it the responsibility of the one who saw clearly, or of those who failed to support the visionary? Is the failure in not seeing or in fearing to trust? Is it an inability to catch hold of something new, or a reluctance to let go of the familiar?

In our personal lives and in our lives in church and society, we need the gifts of those who see far. We need courage to dare to look at the unfamiliar and frightening. We need to live creatively in the tension that may be present where two differing visions intersect.

Each person's vision of life matters. Each person is called to see far and to walk in the light. Each of us needs the message of the lives of those who have seen farther. We are called to reflect on the qualities of the men and women of vision who have gone before us, men and women who, because they had made the lonely inner journey, did not abandon their costly gift of seeing.

We are about to enter into the 21st century and into the third millennium of Christianity. In the small personal communities in which we live, and in the complex and power-oriented world that surrounds us, we need the presence of those whose vision is faithful and prophetic. Unless we nourish both the vision and the visionary who can mold and give direction to human history, we may become its victims. We cannot hope to do this on a national or worldwide scale if we fail to do it in our daily lives. For many of the same reasons that we do not cherish the gift of seeing today, it was a gift not cherished in Jesus.

> The Word was the true light
> that enlightens all men;
> and he was coming into the world.

He was in the world
that had its being through him,
and the world did not know him.
He came to his own domain
and his own people did not accept him.

John 1:9-11

We are reminded of the words of George Bernard Shaw in *Joan of Arc,* "Must good men and women in every age perish to save those who have no imagination?" We know of God's promise in the words of Joel 3:1, "Your sons and daughters shall prophesy, your old men shall dream dreams, and your young men see visions." It is a promise repeated through all of the Hebrew scriptures. Our sadness is misdirected if we believe that God is not keeping that promise, for the promise is faithful and clear. The real sadness is not even that we do not recognize the visionary among us, for I believe we do. The sadness is that we so fear what listening to and following the person of vision will ask of us that we immediately search for reasons for refusing to see what the visionary sees. I believe we do this because our inner insecurities and fears haunt us. We are not sure of our own vision. If we were, the vision of another would pose no threat to us. This is a matter of inner integrity and clarity of personal convictions. It is an experience of the companion I call loneliness.

Recognizing the visionary person for whom seeing is a way of life

The visionary is a light-bearer, one who is willing to pay the price for walking where others may be afraid to follow. This does not mean that the light was easily discovered or that it was not mixed with darkness.

The visionary relies on the belief that the vision is a gift from God and not of one's own making. Such belief means that one has been attentive to inner obstacles to hearing and seeing. It asks a stance toward life that is repentant, and seeks forgiveness. At the same time it recognizes a personal emptiness needing to be filled and a brokenness needing to be healed.

The visionary knows from experience the price of seeing. To be called to see is one of the clearest calls not only to accept suffering as a way of life but to embrace it as did the "Word who was the true light." The hopefulness of the visionary flows out of a central Christian mystery present in all of Jesus' life and teaching.

Because of personal faithfulness and commitment to that which is at the center, the visionary sees clearly that which is at the growing edge.

The vision matters not only to the one who sees, but also to the community being called to follow and share the vision. There is care for others; there may not be freedom from suffering.

The visionary knows that there is no final resting place for any vision being followed. The ongoing listening, reshaping, and sometimes letting go of one vision to fashion a new and more life-giving one is no easy situation in which to find Christ's peace.

So rooted in God's love and faithfulness is the visionary that others are challenged to accept that same love and belief. It is these roots that make it possible for the person of vision to see the connections between persons, things and events. We are not called to independent existence but to life in community. Seeing well means that we take responsibility for the impact of our way of living on the lives of others.

The visionary does not lose sight of the importance of each individual life. A part of the interconnectedness of life reminds us of the simple fact that if by our way of seeing and living we are not contributing to the pool of goodness, then we are strengthening the power of evil.

The visionary is not afraid to walk directly into life with eyes wide open, is not afraid to see reality, and is not afraid to listen to life.

Visionaries, in Paul's words to the Corinthians, have not allowed their minds to be dulled. They have not put a veil over their minds or visions. To see, and to reflect to others the truth of what one sees, does not allow for the seeming security of veiling either mind or heart. The visionary seeks a place of life, not one of easy comfort:

> Do not believe that he who seeks to comfort you lives untroubled among the simple and quiet words that sometimes do you good. His life has much sadness and difficulty. . . . Were it otherwise he would never have been able to find those words.[1]

Every Christian is called to be a pilgrim, a person whose journey is never complete. We are like the early Followers of the Way, a people called to shape and follow a vision. But some are called by God to a quality of seeing that demands more, that cannot be separated from loneliness.

The loneliness of the pilgrim of the future: Teilhard de Chardin

At every period in history some have appeared who received the call to walk in light and to search for direction for themselves and others. Not every one receiving that call had the courage to follow it, for darkness may be more apparent than light.

The visionary is like a pilgrim of two worlds, an inner world of ideas, and an outer world where ideas become reality. Bringing these worlds together is a part of the burden of the gift of seeing. Such a pilgrim, pursuing a vision that may see both farther and differently, may feel at home in no place.

Such a visionary was the Jesuit priest, Teilhard de Chardin. A man who made important contributions to the world of science through his worldwide travel in pursuit of the knowledge of the origins and history of the human race, he was destined to be in exile all of his life.

He often spoke of himself as a "pilgrim of the future" while he lived with the lonely realization that he walked in thought, in faith and in conviction where others before him had never gone. He died on Easter Sunday 1955, and subsequently his vast collection of manuscripts was published. The extent to which he saw into the future was revealed through essays and treatises on a variety of political and social issues: building world community, the repercussions of nuclear energy, exploring life on other planets, the dignity and rights of the human person, the transformation of both the feminine and masculine in human life, respect for life in all of its forms, and the pursuit of peace.

Two central values form an important thread in all his work. The first is reflected in his own words that "The spiritual value of a man, the range of his influence, depends on the degree of reality that God has assumed for him." A goal for which he worked was that the pursuit of every human science and of every principle of the gospel would bring the world community to that place where God is the central reality.

The second value is the recognition of Christ as the alpha and omega of the evolution of the human family. His theory of creation revolves around the relationship of the whole evolutionary process to Christ. It was a costly theory to which he would cling tenaciously; a theory for which he could find no scientific verification.

In an essay written in 1916 he reveals a unique understanding of the Incarnation and of the centrality of Christ's place in the universe:

> The Incarnation is a renewal and a restoration of all the
> forces and powers of the universe; Christ is the instrument,

the centre, the end of all animate and material creation; by Him all things are created, sanctified, made alive. . . .

And since the time when Jesus was born, when He finished growing and died and rose again, everything has continued to move because Christ has not yet completed His own forming. He has not yet gathered in to Himself the last folds of the Garment of flesh and love which His disciples are making for Him. The mystical Christ has not yet attained His full growth. In the pursuance of this engendering is situated the ultimate spring of all creative activity. . . . Christ is the Fulfillment even of the natural evolution of beings.[2]

In his relentless pursuit of these two tenets of his faith, he worked tenaciously to destroy the matter-spirit dichotomy that has haunted both Christian life and scholarship. Like Paul in Corinthians, he believed that we are called to remove whatever veils our minds and hearts so that we may see a vision of life that is adequate to give direction to the ongoing evolution of the human psyche. Like Paul, he saw that in the "groaning of creation" (Rom 8) it is ourselves as well as Christ who are being fulfilled. Like Paul, he reveals the meaning of his own life as he proclaims that love is the only energy in the world, God's love for us, ours for God in Christ, and our love for one another.

The gifts of his vision

To enter fully into the vision of this "pilgrim of the future" requires a study of his thought and of his writings. To share in his spiritual legacy asks us to make a commitment to do in our lives what he spent a lifetime doing. He said, "Seeing . . . I believe that the whole of life consists in that verb—if not ultimately, at least essentially."[3] To reflect on the qualities of his life out of which his vision grew is to strengthen our own desire to follow the vision that we see and to respect the vision of others.

Many who ponder the life of this exiled and lonely pilgrim find richness in his thought and words. We are challenged in different ways and called to greater life through any one or many of his ideas including the following:

1. There is a never-finished dimension to the life of each person and of the human family. As evolution continues, we are the only species that can give direction to our own psychic and physical evolution.

2. Truth converges. Ideas, once born, are never lost. It is enough for truth to come into just one single mind and, the more powerful the truth, the more surely it will spread until it brings light to the world.

3. No light is given to us for ourselves alone. We are called to share the light that we receive and, when we do, the light rekindles itself in us.

4. Some words of Bernanos penned in his notebook reveal his willingness to walk in the midst of misunderstanding while never losing the commitment to what he saw: "Every spiritual adventure is a calvary. . . ."

5. He believed in the connectedness of all things and considered love as the binding force of the universe. Out of the tremendous optimism that he carried for the human family, he took for granted the achieving of world community and the pursuit of the relatedness of all that exists in the entire universe. His simple words were often profound in their implication: "Christ binds us and reveals us to one another."

6. His commitment to pursuing the questions that grew out of his finely tuned powers of observation and listening made him a questioner who caused great inconvenience to church scholars and leaders. Because many of his questions touched on areas believed to be sensitive, he was forbidden to

teach and to publish during his lifetime. This deprived him of the opportunity to refine and reshape his own way of seeing. But his tenacious faithfulness to the questions he formed and followed demonstrated the truth of the motto found on the coat of arms of the de Chardin family: *Igneus est illis vigor et caelestis origo.* (Fiery is their vigor, and of heaven their source.)

7. His poetic *Hymn to Matter* reveals the goodness of matter and its relationship to the meaning of the Incarnation. It reveals our call to cherish our own flesh and human spirit as we grow more like Christ and become the word of God in the world as Jesus did.

8. The important place of the Eucharist in his life is expressed in a recurring way in his work. *The Mass on the World* is a manifestation of the all-inclusive nature of the Eucharist for him. It is also a statement of his awareness of his smallness that needs to be enlarged by God and of his emptiness waiting to be filled by God. His is a call to meet one another in love and friendship as we approach the Eucharist, aware that we are there at God's invitation. He seeks, in the Eucharist, the strength needed to sustain his life in the frequent separations from those he loved: "In every Breaking of the Bread, where it is always Easter, I look for you."

9. For all the complexity of life that he observed, and even in his awareness of the potentially destructive elements in society, he expressed a tender sensitivity for and belief in the sacredness of the human person. Nowhere was it better expressed than in his statement that "Every person is an irreplaceably precious gift."

Neither he nor any of his contemporaries could have envisioned that this pilgrim, exiled in thought and expression even from a church he loved, would have found his vision so frequently expressed in the documents of the Second Vatican Council. Often the words resembled his so much as to sound as if he had written them. During his lonely and costly journey with a vision not seen and never before expressed, who could have predicted that Pope John XXIII would complain not of his content but only of the difficulty of his writing? Only a short time later Pope Paul VI stated: "Father Teilhard is an indispensable man for our times; his expression of faith is necessary for us."

While he lived he was denied the forum in which to test and refine his ideas, and was challenged for the ways in which he crossed disciplinary lines to fashion his synthesis. Yet the impact that his thought holds for those who continue to trust his way of seeing is incalculable.

He veiled neither what he saw nor the expression of the truth of it. Such a vision could have been lost in a man who sought to guard and keep it safe by not sharing it. It could also have been lost by forgetting that it is God's vision, discovered if we walk in light with unveiled minds and hearts.

It could have been lost if Teilhard feared the loneliness of seeing and believing what no one else saw.

But his greatest gift is none of these things. We have yet to speak of the greatest challenge offered by this man dedicated to and willing to pay the price for seeing.

His greatest gift is his invitation to see as Jesus saw and then to stand where Jesus stood. Jesus often saw that values sometimes seem to stand in opposition to one another. He often stood in the lonely and uncomfortable place of seeking to reconcile the seemingly irreconcilable. What Jesus did so perfectly and so masterfully, even in the presence of his most bitter critics and cruelest enemies, is what Teilhard was called to do.

Throughout his life, two values most central in his response to walk in light were his faithfulness to his priesthood and church, and his faithfulness to his ever-emerging vision. He stood as an obedient son of a church that would not allow him to teach or publish because his vision was not trusted. Yet he continued to nourish that vision because faithfulness to himself demanded he do so.

Only those closest to him know the anguish and loneliness which never turned into bitterness. Only his scholarly and personal discipline, his constant pursuit of prayer, and the presence of friends with whom he could share his way of seeing sustained him in his inner certainty that his vision was faithful to the church and to himself. In the face of his fiery and challenging vision others chose to veil their hearts and minds.

His was the spirit of a man who trusted the light he followed, knowing that it was of God. It is a vision that has its roots in the power of his thought and in the courage of his convictions. His own words describe well his spiritual legacy:

> What paralyzes life is the failure to believe and the failure to dare. What is difficult is not solving problems, but formulating them; as we see it now, harnessing passion to make it serve the spirit must . . . be a condition of progress. Therefore, sooner or later, despite our incredulity, the world will take that step. For everything that is more true does come about, and everything that is better is finally achieved. Some day, after mastering the winds, the waves, the tides, and gravity, we shall harness—for God—the energies of love. And then, for the second time in the history of the world, man will have discovered fire.[4]

1. *Letters to a Young Poet*, Rainer Maria Rilke (New York: W.W. Norton Company, 1954).
2. *The Future of Man*, Teilhard de Chardin (New York: Harper & Row, 1964).
3. *Phenomenon of Man*, Teilhard de Chardin (New York: Harper & Row, 1959).
4. *Teilhard de Chardin*, Claude Cuenot (Baltimore: Helicon, 1965) from his essay on "The Evolution of Chastity."

VIII
Embracing the human condition

We are only earthenware jars that hold this treasure, to make it clear that such an overwhelming power comes from God and not from us. We are in difficulties on all sides, but never cornered; we see no answer to our problems, but never despair; we have been persecuted, but never deserted; knocked down, but never killed; always, wherever we may be, we carry with us in our body the death of Jesus, so that the life of Jesus, too, may always be seen in our body. Indeed, while we are still alive, we are consigned to death every day, for the sake of Jesus, so that in our mortal flesh the life of Jesus, too, may be openly shown. So death is at work in us, but life in you.

2 Corinthians 4:7-12

Over the past five years, during a life of continual travel, I have spent numerous hours in airports. Because I can think of few places that symbolize greater loneliness, I have devised several airport games to occupy the seemingly endless times. In one I try to match how a person looks with who they are and what their life history is.

Two years ago I was waiting for a connecting flight at Chicago's O'Hare Airport. My attention was drawn to a medium-tall, well-dressed and rather distinguished-looking gentleman who approached the desk to request his boarding pass. He appeared to be about 70 years old. A melancholy kind of look about him held my interest.

The usual questions flooded my mind as I continued to observe his posture, his manner of walking as he left the desk and the boarding area where I was sitting. I wondered about his family, what kind of parents he had, how many brothers and sisters, where he had lived, what he had done, and what he enjoyed. Most of all, I wondered if the melancholy look

was a signal of deep personal sadness, the result of some painful tragedy in his life.

Soon it was boarding time. It was my great gift that this
man and I had been assigned adjacent aisle and window
seats. He said hello in the manner people usually do when
they sit next to someone on a plane. While making an effort
to hide my heightened curiosity about him, I hoped that we
might get into some comfortable conversation during the two
and a half-hour flight. I decided I would spend time with the
book I had while trying to devise some gentle way of in-
itiating a conversation. The book was a recent gift, one that
greatly interested me. It was *The Book of Clowns* by George
Speaight, a very large book, conspicuous for the large and
clear title on its cover.

As I began to read about the early history of clowns and
clowning I somehow detected this man's interest. My obvious
involvement in the book indicated by the many marginal
notes I was making, led us quite naturally into a conversation
in which he shared with me the story of his life.

His interest in the book was understandable. His father
had been a circus clown. He spoke of his earliest years as a
happy time, living in a community of circus folk and being
loved in such a way that he felt as though he had several sets
of parents caring for him. His father had an unfading sense of
dedication to the importance of the clown in the lives of all
who came to the circus. His father died when he was young,
of a broken heart, he claimed, when his mother abandoned
them and was never seen again.

After his father's death he was taken, somewhat against
his will, from the circus and placed in a foster home. It was
his good fortune that the home was one where he was loved
and with parents who would provide him with a good education. Years later, after the deaths of both his foster parents
and the tragic accidental death of his wife, the memory of his

father and of other dedicated circus entertainers led him back to the circus in search of the meaning his father had found there.

He described for me how easily he had acquired the spirit of the clown as he sought not only practical skills but also some knowledge of the history of clowning and the life stories of some world-famous clowns.

He reminded me that the clown was not the invention of any one nation or culture. The clown, whether in the appearance of court jester, fool, trickster or mimer, has always held an important place and met an important need in society. The clown expresses a vision of life and a way of looking at the world that is at once compelling and freeing. Behind the funny and exaggerated costume and the painted face is an intense person whose own experience of the intensity of life calls him to bring the release of comedy to children and adults alike.

He told me that the best clowns are those with far-seeing and creative spirits; the best clowns are the unconventional thinkers who free others and encourage them to find new ways in which to look at both themselves and their world. The use of makeup and costume, linked with the convincingly indomitable spirit of the gifted clown, is a powerful means of helping others to see the humor in the incongruities of human life.

He spoke in a very moving way about the loneliness in his father's life after his mother had disappeared. And he spoke of the intensity of his own loneliness. It had been one of the primary reasons for his rejoining the circus late in his life. He somehow wanted to make people laugh, to help them forget, even if only for a short time, about whatever sadness they carried.

We read together the following quotation from *The Book of Clowns:*

In private life, clowns are not funny men; they are often reserved, often sad and lonely. Perhaps the ultimate appeal of the clown lies in this double image. When they don the motley they become agents of a great reversal of everything that is taken for granted in ordinary life. They may be tricked, beaten and humiliated, but in their hands these things become matters for laughter, and the sadness of life is transformed. To see a great clown is, for a child or a philosopher, wonderful too. The world is turned upside down. In the words of Henry Miller, "Clowns and angels meet together."[1]

The parallels between that passage and the words of Paul in 2 Corinthians must not remain unnoticed: "We are in difficulties on all sides but we never despair; knocked down, but never killed; we carry all this with us in our bodies."

Too soon it was time for us to land. This sad-eyed man in sharing his own story had not only reviewed for me the meaning and role of the clown, he had also led me into further reflection on the universal messages about human life that are inherent in the meaning of clowning.

As we left the plane and were walking into the jetway my retired clown companion handed me a card. On it were his name, address and phone number. Under that, penned in his own hand were the words, "I am Barnabas, the Clown." I did not look at the card until after we had parted and mail sent to him is returned to me unclaimed. I cannot verify, though I am sure that his name must have been selected carefully and in relation to the brief words in Acts 4:36-37: "There was a Levite of Cypriot origin called Joseph whom the apostles surnamed Barnabas (which means 'son of encouragement')."

The marks of the clown: The signs of encouragement

The presence of this melancholy man persists. There is a meaning in that meeting, however brief it was, that cannot be explained by my own studied and somewhat philosophical interest in clowns. Neither is it related solely to the thoughtful kind of man he was.

After long periods of personal reflection I have concluded that the clown, more than any other kind of actor, artist or entertainer, is the one who best mediates to us the meaning of a fully human life and then goes beyond that to invite us to feel at home in the human condition. One of the great services that the clown renders is to so release us from the destructive intensity with which we pursue life that we relax into being who we are—flesh and blood and filled with incongruities. The clown is a graced and gracing presence for us in encouraging us to cherish being what we most are—human. Continual reflection on the humanness of Jesus involves us in accepting as a given the humanness that Jesus chose:

> His state was divine
> yet he did not cling
> to his equality with God
> but emptied himself . . .
> and became as men are;
> and being as all men are,
> he was humbler yet,
> even to accepting death,
> death on a cross.
> But God raised him high
> and gave him the name
> which is above all names. . . .
>
> Philippians 2:6-9

The creative ability of clowns is manifested in their ability to lead us into laughter. Christopher Fry, in his play *The Lady's Not for Burning*, tells us that "Laughter is the surest touch of genius in creation." The profound meaning of this touches me most when I think of the people I have known who temporarily lost their ability to laugh. A sign of their healing is the gradual reclaiming of the gift of laughter.

We live in a society which badly needs the clown's presence and the gift of laughter. I am reminded of this in surprising and sometimes unexpected ways. One such way happened on a Saturday morning a few months ago. I was making my journey down Beacon Street with a very large bag of laundry needing attention.

I looked up to see Miss Piggy approaching (or at least someone wearing a Miss Piggy mask). I was so delighted that I put down my laundry bag to look, to smile and to laugh. Miss Piggy's response was not long in coming as the young woman removed her mask and told me I had made her day. She told me that she had walked several blocks and met dozens of people, none of whom had smiled or allowed themselves to respond in any way.

Even in a city as unusual as Boston, I am disappointed that so many passers-by were not able to receive the gift of that playful young woman, the gift of laughter she wanted to share.

Laughter provides us with an opportunity not unlike the release of human moods while experiencing the varying movements in a well-performed symphony.

Laughter bears a transcending power, an infectious force, that carries us beyond our preoccupation with some pain or suffering and leads us, however briefly, into some brighter place. It takes us outside ourselves for a moment. It gives us some distance, in order to regain perspective and again to set things in focus.

Laughter is a manifestation of love and care. With friends it expresses faithful love. Among enemies, where we do not easily laugh, it has sometimes broken down barriers.

Laughter is a gift we can choose to give to one another, even when we are hurting or lonely. Every good clown gives living witness to the importance of this gift for one who would be, like my friend, Barnabas, a "son of encourage-ment."

The nature of the stance that a clown takes reminds us of the humanizing gift of vulnerability. Precisely because the clown places himself in the position of powerlessness, he is vulnerable to others. Out of this vulnerability he reminds us that the power of loving flows out of our willingness to love even though we may be hurt in the act of openly offering love. Because the clown consistently refuses to accept the limits of the possible he reminds us that we ought not set limits on our ability to give and receive faithful love.

The vulnerability of the clown is a countersign in a culture which places great value on both security and success. The clown can lead us to see that a willingness to be vulnerable before others is the graced and chosen gift at the center of every choice for new or renewed life. The lonely cost of this approach to life explains why this message of the life of the clown is often not valued by superficial observers.

Whatever pain is present in the life of a clown, he does not allow it to make him a self-centered person, a person who turns in on life, to nurse and cling to the pain. Because the clown is self-forgetful, and manifests that in his dress and ac-tion, his reaching out to others distracts them from an ex-cessive preoccupation with their own lives.

The clown sometimes carries heavily the personal pain that is a part of his life. Yet he offers life to others in such an undemanding way that his audience is able to grasp a vision of reality wider than their own and to share in the lives of others in some unpredicted way. Because he is disarmingly unassuming, he is allowed entrance into lives less open than his own.

By alerting us to life in unique and laughter-filled ways, the clown invites us to both look and see in ways we might previously have feared. Through his encouragement, our world is enlarged and made to seem more amiable. Through that same encouragement we sense that the refusal to risk for life is no mark of success; that the fear of making mistakes, if acted on, will make us less than human.

It is in risking that we find release from the difficult and unanswered questions of life. When we choose to risk even what we are, for what we are called to be, we enter into the paradox which Jesus, in his own vulnerable stance toward life, chose as his way. It is the way of which Paul speaks:

> Do you see now how God has shown up the foolishness of human wisdom? If it was God's wisdom that human wisdom should not know God, it was because God wanted to save those who have faith through the foolishness of the message that we preach. And so, while the Jews demanded miracles and the Greeks look for wisdom, here are we preaching a crucified Christ; to the Jews an obstacle that they cannot get over, to the pagans madness, but to those who have been called, whether they are Jews or Greeks, a Christ who is the power and the wisdom of God. For God's foolishness is wiser than human wisdom, and God's weakness is stronger than human strength.
>
> 1 Corinthians 1:21-25

A quality of many of our lives is a propensity to take both ourselves and our world much too seriously. If we make a life-and-death issue of every human circumstance, if we see every small obstacle as if it were larger than life, we would soon lack the ability to distinguish between the fine print and the headlines. We would soon be no longer able to discern where it is and in what ways we catch hold of the meaning of life. We would also reject the words of Paul that are an invitation to notice the difference between the life of Jesus and our own; to notice the difference between Jesus' approach to life and our own.

The clown, while releasing us from the intensity of life

through laughter and through ever-present encouragement to accept our human skins, refuses the role of the magician while continually leading us into the mystery of the reality of life. He would not use magic to cheat us even of our discomfort. His message is one of a continual enjoyment of life. One of the beautiful enticements of the clown is his own entering into and enjoyment of the fun he makes for us.

In the era of clowning that goes back to the origins of the Feast of Fools, the clown was given a special place and was even revered as one possessed by God. One particular quality speaks to this special place of clowns—that is their commitment to remind us, by their presence, that one who hurts can help to heal others. Their presence is a reminder that it is possible to transcend one's own pain because one sees and cares about the pain of another. And, clowns through all ages, by being present to both the hurting and the happy in the crowd, have not found escape from their loneliness and suffering. But they have found meaning in life. The response and especially the laughter of the crowds gives encouragement to the Barnabas of the circus. Our laughter continually frees the clown to embrace his own humanness so that he can continue to be there for us.

> Big boots, floppy clothes,
> Painted face, button nose,
> That's Johnny the Clown.
>
> .   .   .
>
> Who says thanks for all the laughter,
> Gives you hugs and kisses after?
> Johnny, are you lonely, too?
>
> Comic smile, goggle eyes,
> Who knows if he laughs or cries?
> Just Johnny—Johnny the Clown.[2]

Does not one of the most frightening dimensions of human pain lie in the lonely feeling that we hurt and no one else knows or cares? Does not much of our loneliness manifest itself in the poignant moment when we wonder, "Who knows if I laugh or cry?"

In the transcending of their own pain, the clowns lead us to fuller life.

> Yet the great clowns, whether of circus or stage or screen, are more than just funny. They bear in their bodies the scars of the human tragedy, reminding us that comedy is a further step, an escape in the direction of Life.[3]

The life of the clown as much as his performance turns loss into gain, exchanges sadness for laughter, and rescues us from the lonely darkness of the human condition while leading us further into the meaning of life. The role of the clown is the role of a Jesus of Nazareth. The marks the clown bears are the signs of encouragement to which Jesus continually calls us. The circus call that goes out in times of tragedy to "send in the clowns" has its roots with a God whose own version of that call was proclaimed in the Word made flesh.

Jesus: The marked clown

Jesus, in his acceptance of God's call to be the Word made flesh, is the Barnabas who most encouraged the early Followers of the Way to believe that it was in and through their human lives, faithfully lived, that they would come closer to Yahweh. The people of Jesus' time so feared the way of the human that the earliest heresy in Christianity was not a denial of the divinity of Jesus but the refusal to accept him as God made man.

Through all his life Jesus embodied the suffering servant songs found in Isaiah, songs prophetic of how he would be present to, and live among, his people as one of them and as one called to serve them. The suffering servant's words reflect Jesus' own acceptance of being flesh and blood as we are:

"Yahweh called me before I was born, from my mother's womb" (Is 49:1) and "Yahweh has given me a disciple's tongue. So that I may know how to reply to the wearied he provides me with speech" (Is 50:4).

It is unfortunate that we do not find revealed in the pages of sacred scripture the profound sense of humor that Jesus must have had. Surviving with his followers, most especially the 12 with whom he walked most closely, could not have been possible without the laughter which best frees us from the destructiveness of life's incongruities. We find, in some of the parables, and in the recounting of other stories about Jesus, only traces of the tongue in cheek and the playful. If the humor was clearer, and it must have been, it has been masked by the intensity of the writers and their choice of words, or perhaps through the series of translations in which the subtlety of humor could easily be lost.

I believe his claim that he had come as servant and friend, not as lord and master, was best revealed in his most powerful and empowering act of service to us—that of accepting what it meant to be human and inviting us to do as he had done.

Those who have portrayed Jesus as a clown figure portray him as a man whose life was exemplified by many of the marks of the clown. The clowns who follow Jesus realize that they, like Jesus, are called to live lives that are marked by suffering and sometimes scarred in the process of living. Like Jesus and all who are marked to be his followers, "God has put his apostles at the end of his parade, with the men sentenced to death" (1 Cor 4:9).

The message of Jesus is clear. It is only in being fully human that we can come to the fullness of life. Even more than accepting them, we are called to cherish and embrace the marks of our humanness. And, as this invitation to life is clear, so is its reward. It is the reward we receive when we, like Barnabas, share life with others. In so doing, we reveal its goodness to them. The message of Jesus for those who do this offers encouragement because it is the message of a loving God who believes that to be human is the greatest gift one can receive. When we, too, have become the Word made flesh we shall understand the meaning of Yahweh's promise:

> Yahweh is an everlasting God,
> he created the boundaries of the earth.
> He does not grow tired or weary,
> his understanding is beyond fathoming.
> He gives strength to the wearied,
> he strengthens the powerless.
> Young men grow tired and weary,
> youths may stumble,
> but those who hope in Yahweh renew their strength,
> they put out wings like eagles.
> They run and do not grow weary,
> walk and never tire.
>
> Isaiah 40:28-31

1. *The Book of Clowns*, George Speaight (New York: Macmillan, 1980).
2. *The Clowns of God*, Morris West (New York: William Morrow and Company, 1981).
3. *The Clown and the Crocodile*, Joseph C. McClelland (Richmond, Va.: John Knox Press, 1970).

IX
Calling each other to life

A disciple called Ananias who lived in Damascus had a vision in which he heard the Lord say to him, "Ananias!" When he replied, "Here I am, Lord," the Lord said, "You must go to Straight Street and ask at the house of Judas for someone called Saul, who comes from Tarsus. At this moment he is praying, having had a vision of a man called Ananias coming in and laying hands on him to give him back his sight."

Acts 9:10-12

I have always had respect for the sacredness of the teaching profession. The roots of this respect were set early in my life, for my father was a teacher. Later on I chose to become a teacher. Some of the most important people in my life have been teachers who called me to life by sharing much more than their professional ability with me.

My father never exerted any sort of pressure on us to become teachers, though he encouraged all of us to do something worthwhile with our lives, something that would make a difference to more than just ourselves.

Looking back on my life I realize that only a few teachers influenced me greatly, whether in or out of school. Some of my teachers were present for me in less important ways. Though I cannot even remember all of their names, the words of Pozzo in *Waiting for Godot* somehow apply to each of them: "The more people I meet the happier I become." From every teacher I departed wiser, richer, more conscious of my blessings.

One of the important things about good teachers is that what we learn from them stays with us through all our lives. What we learn is with us to strengthen and give encouragement, especially in lonely moments and at turning points. Because good teachers offer us life without imposing it, and receive what we have to give without demanding anything from us, they help us to become who we are. They remain with us as we walk with the loneliness inevitably resulting from choices that are faithful to whom we can become.

It is the gift of the good teacher to be attentive to each person. This attentiveness and sensitivity make the teacher vulnerable because one who offers presence can be rejected or ignored. The teacher who stands in that place knows the loneliness of waiting, watching and listening with another without the ability to foresee the response.

Some people feel it is enough to live by a concept expressed well by Woody Allen: "Eighty percent of life is in showing up." But the people I consider to have been teachers not only showed up, but more importantly, were present to their lives and mine. They taught me this not by words, but by the manner in which they gave me the message that growth in life has a quality of mutuality that makes the medium the message.

Listening to my own life has taught me that, sometimes when I feel lonely in a particularly intense or painful way, it is because I am inattentive to the presence of people who could be there for me. I also know that my sense of loneliness is related to my carelessness in making the effort to be present to whomever I am with.

Questions addressed to Jesus often began with the word "rabbi" which means "teacher." One such question and Jesus' response carries with it great meaning for me because it reveals the teacher in Jesus, the teacher who continually offers an invitation but provides no clear explanation of how the invitation is to be followed. And so it was when they came to Jesus:

Hearing this, the two disciples followed Jesus. Jesus turned around, saw them following and said, "What do you want?" They answered, "Rabbi"—which means Teacher—"where do you live?" "Come and see" he replied.

John 1:38-39

Like Jesus, the teachers who have been most helpful to me are those who offered life, or who opened doors through which I might choose to walk. They neither did it for me, nor did they tell me exactly how I should fashion my response. The challenge to the teacher is to know when to be present, in what way and just how much.

Jesus was a master at this. He called others to a life that could be lived neither superficially nor halfheartedly. This was the gentle Jesus who called his followers to a quality of life they could never have sought or attained had it not been for his presence to them. He calls us to that same life through his ongoing presence in both the word and the bread which is Eucharist. What other teacher would ever dare call his followers to "eat his flesh and drink his blood"? What other teacher could say, "Follow me and make my values your own to such an extent and in such a way that you become me"?

When I think about teachers who have been important to me, one person surfaces in my memory more often than others. She was a farseeing visionary in the church long before Vatican II was ever thought of; she was a liberated woman with no feminists around to sow the seeds in her mind. I remember her equally for her abundance of common sense as well as her brilliance. She was a teacher in whose composition and journalism classes I frequently heard, "You can do this better. Write it again." And so I did and so I learned.

I stand in awe of and yet as friend of this woman. Perhaps I have idealized her through the years. Perhaps she has become the embodiment of the qualities that were important enough to me that I, as a teacher, hoped to make them my own. I do know that she continues to be mentor and challenger to me, a woman whose presence in my life enables me to become some of what she continues to believe I can be. She does not let me rest in mediocrity.

It was an awesome thing when this woman I so admire asked me to autograph one of my books for her. Only someone of her stature and grace would leave so tender a note: "Your book is on my bedstand. It will mean so much more to me if you would write a message in it for me."

Her way of being present to me has shown itself at countless times throughout the years that we have walked together, first as teacher and student and then as members of the same Franciscan family. Her name is Sister Mileta Ludwig.

The year I entered the community she was transferred from the high school I attended in Spokane, Washington, to St. Rose Convent. We went to LaCrosse, Wisconsin, the same year. In those first lonely weeks and months, it was she more than any other who encouraged me and guided me. It was she who made my lonely days brighter by her own sharing of the times of loneliness she had known.

Each year since, she has grown closer to me as a mentor. She offers me the assurance that she stands beside me, caring and supporting. She also respects me enough to set me free and to avoid giving advice even when she does not understand the decisions I make. While generously sharing her wisdom, she has allowed me to make my own mistakes.

I cherish this woman in a special way now. Who she is and how she has lived her life are clearer to me now than ever. Her ability to share the insights of a brilliant mind and a loving heart are made increasingly difficult for her because she is now legally blind and her hearing worsens with the passing of each day. She shares with me the lonely agony of this way in which reading and writing have become impossible. Even carrying on a conversation is now an exhausting process. By her example she continues to teach me about the meaning of life. She invites me to walk with loneliness as she does, in whatever mysterious and unforeseen ways it comes into our lives.

Few people have the gift of sharing such a long part of the journey with so gifted a teacher. Few people have had a faithful teacher stand beside them in such life-giving ways. A favorite story of mine illustrates well some of the ways in which Mileta has called me to discover life by sharing her life with me.

The story of the artist and the little boy

This story, which had its roots in a poverty-stricken area of Harlem, has undergone many transformations for me through my own retelling of it. It is no longer clear to me nor does it really matter how the story has changed or in what ways. It is like Lillian Hellman's interpretation of *pentimento* as the ways in which "the old conception, replaced by a later choice, is a way of seeing and then seeing again."

A priest friend was transferred from a suburban parish to one in the heart of Harlem. On arriving in his new place, he discovered a church and a neighborhood that were in a physical disarray that reflected well the lack of care and community among the poor and the powerless who survived there. Because he cared about what he found, his dream was to find some way to bring people together and to help establish bonds among themselves out of which would grow the kind of support they needed. Realizing that he did not know how to help them develop the leadership and skills they needed to do this, he sought help from others in similar kinds of neighborhoods.

While he was making different attempts to bring the people together, he was visited by an artist friend who had some experience with people suffering from this kind of oppression. He said, "It is not important that they talk to you. What is important is that you get them talking to one another. They need to begin to share their stories in order to begin to trust each other."

Volunteering his skills as an artist and some experiences that had worked for him, he suggested it would be helpful to involve people in making collages and pictures that would tell their stories. And so one evening the artist brought together a large group of children from the neighborhood. Each child received a felt-tip marker and some large poster paper. After making some pictures for them that told his story, he invited them to make some pictures that would tell each other about their homes and families. He captured their imaginations sufficiently so that at first a few and then most of the children were busy making pictures of their parents, their brothers and sisters, their cat or dog. To his delight, they seemed eager to say as much about themselves and their homes and families as they could.

As the artist walked among them, he noticed a boy about 11 sitting looking at the paper. He was silent and drawing nothing. The artist stood beside the boy, silent and attentive. He felt the little boy looking at his feet, but not looking up at him. He continued to stand there and, finally the little boy looked up, but said nothing. When the artist had the feeling that something had happened between them, he put out his hand and pointed to the felt-tip marker as a signal for the little boy to give it to him. The artist took the marker and made several wide strokes back and forth across the paper as the boy watched intently. Then the artist turned the paper over, put the marker into the boy's hand and pointed to the paper.

The little boy repeated the same kind of strokes the artist

had made. The artist stood there a few moments, again in silence, replaced the paper with a new one, again put out his hand to receive the marker. This time the artist drew large circles, moving freely and communicating clearly his enjoyment in what he was doing. Then, he turned the paper over and handed the marker back to the little boy and again pointed to the paper. The little boy smiled and repeated the circles, in much the way he had seen the artist make them. The artist sensed some change in the manner of the boy as he took a third piece of paper, put it in front of the boy and simply handed him the marker. The little boy began to make pictures of himself, his sister, and soon was telling his story.

There is in the experience of both the artist and the little boy a place that I can only call loneliness. Each offered what he had as each faced an unknown response. The artist in offering was open to possible misunderstanding and rejection. The boy in allowing another into his life was as vulnerable to the unknown as was the artist. The artist had entered the life of the little boy without clear invitation and found acceptance. The boy accepted the presence of this stranger and found the freedom to tell his story. Both were changed in the process—the artist by the openness and acceptance of the boy; the boy by sharing in an experience beyond his own.

There is in each of us an artist and a little boy. There is in each of us a person who sometimes frees others and is sometimes freed by others. There is in each of us the kind of gift that can only be set free by silent presence, as there is in each of us the ability to free others simply by standing at their side. There is in each of us an artist whose life experience enables us to invite others to life. There is in each of us a child who can grow beyond some point only because another cares enough to share a presence.

There is an interesting sequel to the story. Later, as the

artist recounted the story to the Harlem pastor, he remembered something he had forgotten as he stood beside the boy. He remembered that as a young art student, he had been given a precious canvas which he placed carefully on a stand close to where he painted. He intended to keep that canvas until he was sure he could produce a painting worthy of the precious material. One day, as he painted, his teacher came and stood beside him. Without conversation, the teacher observed the young student. Then, the teacher took the brush from the young artist, turned to the precious canvas, put some strokes across it, returned the brush to the student's hand and pointed to the once unused canvas. And the young student painted a picture which he now considers one of his best works.

Sister Mileta, my parents and others have been present to me and have called me to life as a good teacher does, as Jesus did. They have had a sense of timing about my life that sometimes either eluded me or was unclear. They instinctively knew when silent presence was more effective than words. They also did not hesitate to speak when the time was right. And, in the end, each had a way of communicating to me that I was important to them, too.

Ananias, an inviting presence for Saul

I find a profound parallel between the story of the artist and the little boy and the recounting of the relationship between Saul and Ananias.

A disciple called Ananias who lived in Damascus had a vision in which he heard the Lord say to him, "Ananias!" When he replied, "Here I am, Lord," the Lord said, "You must go to Straight Street and ask at the house of Judas for someone called Saul, who comes from Tarsus. At this moment he is praying, having had a vision of a man called

Ananias coming in and laying hands on him to give him back his sight."

When he heard that, Ananias said, "Lord, several people have told me about this man and all the harm he has been doing to your saints in Jerusalem. He has only come here because he holds a warrant from the chief priests to arrest everybody who invokes your name." The Lord replied, "You must go all the same, because this man is my chosen instrument to bring my name before pagans and pagan kings and before the people of Israel; I myself will show him how much he himself must suffer for my name." Then Ananias went. He entered the house, and at once laid his hands on Saul and said, "Brother Saul, I have been sent by the Lord Jesus who appeared to you on your way here so that you may recover your sight and be filled with the Holy Spirit." Immediately it was as though scales fell away from Saul's eyes and he could see again. So he was baptised there and then, and after taking some food he regained his strength.

Acts 9:10-19

Like the artist, Ananias was sent to be present to Saul and to set him free. Ananias, who had been called by God in a mysterious way and to a fearsome task, was transformed in the process of ministering to Saul in his sightlessness and temporary inactivity.

Saul, like the boy, needed someone to show him the way. He needed to be freed by someone whose life experiences could lead him through the unknown to a place that would become familiar to him.

The story of Saul and Ananias reminds us that we do not free ourselves. Ananias went to Saul because God called him to do that. Through the presence of Ananias, Saul was healed of his sightlessness and was able to see and respond to God's call to him. The story reminds us that without our presence to one another, God's work is not begun or remains unfinished. It reminds us that human conversion is first an experience of persons who stand in relationship to one another so that they are able to allow God to be more present in their lives.

For Saul, this meant a new direction in his life. For Ananias, the response to God's call led him to a deeper place of life in relationship to the Lord. Each had been a place of life for the other. It is ironic that, almost against his will, Saul is reduced to being led by someone else; Ananias reluctantly agrees to lead Saul out of his darkness. Saul questions; Ananias is hesitant. Both respond.

Like the story of the artist and the little boy, Saul's conversion reminds us that in our moments of turning to God, someone stands beside us, invites us, walks with us, and so reminds us of God's freeing presence with us. And both receive the gift of life, though each in a different way.

Giving and receiving life

As we pursue the sometimes lonely journey through our own life experiences, the presence of those who walk with us, without words but with great love, frees us and strengthens us to go on. Those who are free inside themselves set us free from the inner fears and insecurities which paralyze us. Those who have known the cost of beginning and ending give us the courage to somehow do it better or at least to try again.

And the people who do this best convey the clear message that they are walking with us, growing with us and cherishing our presence as a gift to them. They are, for us, the kind of presence that Jesus was for the marginal members of society who found no accepted place at the center; for the misunderstood who carried the heavy burden of the easy judgments righteous people impose on the lives of others; for those whose battered self-images badly needed only the loving affirmation that heals; for the sinful ones who had walked away from God and had no one to bring them the message of loving forgiveness. They are the kind of presence that Mileta has been for me.

As we walk together each person faces life experiences that carry with them the potential to destroy or to lead to greater life. We face experiences that can either paralyze us or set us free. We can choose to open doors to new life or to close them forever. It is the presence of others with us, loving us and reaching out to us that makes it possible for us to trust ourselves. It is the presence of others that encourages us as we walk with loneliness.

There is in each of us a Saul and an Ananias. There is in each of us a presence that sometimes sets others free and sometimes is in need of being set free. Like Saul our eyes are open and yet we see nothing; like Ananias whose eyes were open we sometimes do not see. Like Saul, the natural leader, we are sometimes led by a somewhat unsure Ananias, the faithful follower. We can only wonder how it might have been different for Saul had Ananias refused to go to Straight Street.

Ananias, who had seen the gospel message clearly and had followed it, experienced the loneliness of the uncertainty of his mission to Saul. As he set out to persuade others to follow his newfound way, Saul discovered the loneliness in both seeing and not seeing. For either Ananias or Saul to have refused to walk with the loneliness of insecurity would have been for them to ignore God's call. They would lose the possibility of the inner certainty that can grow only out of such grace-filled moments.

For the artist and the little boy, for Saul and Ananias, and for ourselves, the presence of one who offers not words but hope, who offers a reassurance that neither binds nor induces dependency, who offers no answers but raises the life-giving questions, leaves us all with the rare gift of believing that we have called them to life even as we have followed their call. It is the gifted teacher who assumes this lonely and vulnerable stance before life. In assuming this stance, the teacher sets us free in those lonely moments of inner paralysis when we either do not see or are afraid of what we see.

The good teacher recognizes that we call one another to life in different but equally important ways. It was so for Jesus and it remains so for us as we follow him. Accepting the gifts that someone offers as they simply stand beside me helps transform that person's experience of loneliness and my own. Offering to stand beside and walk with another helps me discover the goodness locked into the mystery of loneliness.

To all of my teachers, but especially to Mileta, I say, "Thank you for sharing God's call to life."

X
Removing the barriers to life

But now in Christ Jesus, you that used to be so far apart have been brought very close by the blood of Christ. For he is the peace between us, and has made the two into one and broken down the barrier that used to keep them apart, actually destroying in his own person the hostility. . . . Later he came to bring the good news of peace, peace to you who were far away and peace to those who were near at hand.

Ephesians 2:13-17

I recently saw a tattered, old placard on the bulletin board in a public building. Its message was not new to me, but the simple statement that "People are lonely because they build walls instead of bridges" set me thinking about some lines of Robert Frost's:

"Something there is that doesn't love a wall. . . .
Before I built a wall, I'd ask to know
What I was walling in or walling out."

Those two quotations led me to give some serious thought to the walls I build and my reasons for setting them so carefully. My first thoughts were of a friend named Teddy Judge, whose life gives little evidence of walls in him that block life from him. My friend of 23 is in a wheelchair and has a speech difficulty. Possessing either disability might tempt me into being a very different kind of person than this lovingly communicative friend.

Teddy has challenged me to try to get inside his world so that my own world is larger. He reminds me of the blind people I meet whose vision of life is larger than mine; of the deaf people whose ability to listen to life is more finely tuned than mine; of the nonspeakers who communicate better nonverbally than I do; and of the others, who in the face of great obstacles, have reached across those barriers to discover a rich and full life.

In thinking about Teddy and the experience of my own life, I wondered how much of my personal loneliness is the result of the inner walls I build and carry with me. I wondered about the walls that block some of the richness of life from me, that block the presence of people who, even if present to me in some way, would be much more present were it not for something inside of me.

It would be a mistake to misuse or misrepresent either quotation. Even in everyday life, from a practical point of view we need both walls and bridges. Though some have tried to interpret Frost's poem to mean that all walls should come down, we do the poet a great disservice if we fail to note the clarity of his thought in saying "something" does not love a wall. There is no implication that "nothing" does. Like the seawalls that protect the land, some are necessary. The key to both lines may lie in Frost's words, "*Before* I built a wall, I'd ask to know what I was walling in or walling out." The poet challenges us here, for we may, in fact, be building walls when we think we are building bridges. And we may not know it for a long time.

My reflections on the two quotations and the challenge presented by Teddy led me to some naming of various kinds of walls. This list is neither exhaustive nor is it arranged in any order of priority or of logic.

Walls observed and unobserved

A wall is a structure serving to enclose, to divide, to support or to protect. This definition serves well both the preceding reflections and those that follow. Unlike the walls we build out of various materials and for specific purposes, often our inner walls, even after we have located them, are not so easily identified in relationship to their impact on ourselves and on those with whom we share life. Even in naming these walls, much of their potential meaning remains unclear.

Walls that are ambiguous. I have had occasion to visit men and women in prison. Once I was visiting a man in a prison where there was continual turmoil and frequent taking of hostages. Each time I entered the visiting area and had keen feelings about the lack of privacy for families and lovers, I thought of how high those walls seemed to the men inside. But one day as I was leaving the prison to walk to my car, I met a woman who lived just down the street from the prison. She told me that she was afraid of the recent difficulties inside and she wished those walls were higher and much more secure. How different those walls are for the person confined by them and for the person living near them.

Walls of indifference. For the person who has adequate food and the luxury of sometimes choosing to fast from food, the problems of the millions who know only starvation and malnutrition can long be ignored. The person in a secure marriage may wonder why couples having problems can't work things out, and why anyone chooses divorce. My friend Teddy sometimes says to me, "Think of it this way, Paula. How would you feel if you were the only person who could walk and everyone else was in a wheelchair?"

Walls of discomfort in the presence of another. In my whole lifetime I have met about half a dozen people whose presence makes me feel as I do when people scratch their fingernails on a blackboard. For some not immediately apparent reason, they create a deep desire in me to be someplace else. That this reveals as much about me as about them is of no practical value. At a later time when I have tracked the feelings, I have sometimes discovered some of my own growing edges in much the same manner one might step on a hot coal hidden in the sand.

The built-in walls of human limitations. No one has all the time, the energy, the ability or whatever to be present to and in the exact manner wanted or needed by every person we meet. It is not a question of either generosity or dedication. We need to remember this in order to deal with the guilt we may experience when we realize that we were not or could not be present to someone in the way they expected us to be. Saying "no, I cannot be there" may not be understood or accepted. But we may have to say no to the pleaser in ourselves in order to say yes to life for ourselves and for those with whom we will walk in the coming days. This is not an easy lesson for those of us who have tricked ourselves into believing that yes is the only faith-filled response acceptable in life.

Walls of deference or respect. The author of *The Little Prince* spoke eloquently of "observing the rites," of approaching with sensitivity and, sometimes, with awe. The home in which I grew up taught me the same lessons. I would never have called my father and my mother, my aunts and uncles or my parents' friends by their first names. There is something in me that believes that there is a certain "grace" with which God endows certain positions and offices—if the people in those positions care enough to bring even a minimum dignity to the office—whether parent or teacher or bishop or friend.

Walls that we choose because we must. Sometimes we need distance and space from friends, from enemies, from people indifferent to us, or from the probing intensity of life. There is a difference between running away from life and choosing the distance that we need in order to enter into life.

It takes a certain kind of life experience to know the difference between running from and running to.

Walls of duplicity. The greatest destructiveness of duplicity manifests itself when we can no longer readily identify the difference between the truth of a situation and what we wish to believe about it. It manifests itself when we no longer realize that we have portrayed a situation a certain way for so long that we no longer know the truth of that situation.

Temporary walls. Counselors speak of them as the defenses we must choose for a period of time in order that life can emerge for us. One such temporary wall is the coping mechanism we call grieving. We speak of such temporary walls when we acknowledge to ourselves that we need time and space.

Subtle or subconscious walls. Perhaps the most destructive walls are those we do not know are there. We have been attentive neither to their building nor to their impact on our lives. They are walls we neither consciously set nor claim as our own. They influence us in ways we claim no responsibility for. Yet they are ours to come to terms with.

Humor as a distancing wall. While acclaiming humor and laughter as an important gift in our lives, I have often been struck by the ways in which I have observed others using humor to keep someone at a safe distance. To respond in jest to someone inviting us to take them seriously manifests a great lack of sensitivity and a refusal to deal with the feelings of another.

Walls of mutual dependence. It is not uncommon for two longtime friends to realize, often through some painful circumstance, that the relationship has grown out of the unrecognized needs of either or both, rather than being based on mutual sharing. Offering to another in friendship the gift of who I am is very different from being dependent on another to determine who I am. This dependence separates rather than unites people.

Walls of compulsive giving. One clear truth about friendship is that both people must be able to give and receive with equal ease. One of the difficult truths about compulsive giving is that often it borders on subtle manipulation. It carries the hidden expectation that the other must respond as I wish because I have given so much. Reflection on how we feel when we give much and the other does not respond the way we hoped, bears messages we might not want to receive about ourselves. We should not hide behind the half-truth that would have us believe that "it is better to give than to receive." The whole truth is that it is important for us to be comfortable in both giving and receiving.

Walls made with words. Reflection on my life and on relationships with others is sometimes a painful reminder of the ways in which words are used too easily or too quickly. A steady flow of words when attentive silence would be more appropriate sets great distances between ourselves and others. The comfortable silence of friends who use words more carefully, and sometimes not at all, tells us about the damage words can do. The memory of an evening watching the mime Marcel Marceau review the beauty and the pain of the human condition is indelible.

Walls of fear and insecurity. One of the mysterious aspects of friendship is, for me, the realization that while I dread saying good-bye to someone I love, I am sometimes equally afraid to say hello. With a friend I have known there is a tendency to look upon time apart as wasted. With a new friend there is an urgency about the desire to know the friend better. Each is sometimes a place of loneliness which manifests itself in either fear or insecurity, perhaps unrecognized or unspoken. It is present nonetheless and not life-giving to the friendship if it goes unnoticed for too long.

The list could continue, and perhaps it will as we reflect on the walls recognizable in ourselves. Webster may serve as the best guide when we examine the walls we have set to determine if they "enclose, divide, support or protect."

Another complicating factor is that I can set walls between myself and the various selves I am, think I am, or would like to be, as well as between myself and God.

Dealing with walls

Robert Frost may be idealistic in his expectation that we can determine what we are walling in and out before we set the wall. Sometimes we can only determine the nature of events and relationships in retrospect. Be that as it may, there are some things that we can do as we seek to deal with our own barrier to life.

We must put to rest the destructive falsehood that we ought have no walls. Some walls, by definition, protect and support. Our own experience of life tells us that to be totally defenseless is folly. Total openness to everyone and everything is as foreign to healthy nature as is the overly cautious approach that protects life to the point of destruction.

I am reminded of the story of a man who made a garden. Realizing that the rabbits and other small animals could harm it, he set a fence around the garden. While the fence protected his garden from the rabbits, it was not high enough to keep out larger animals. So, the next year he again set a wall around his garden and this time it was just the right height to protect his plants. His yield was of good quality and abundant, a great source of pride. The third year, remembering the success of the past he decided that if a wall around the garden had given such good results certainly a wall around each plant would be even better. In his forgetfulness of the place of the wind, the sun and the rain, he destroyed his own garden.

How like that gardener we are in our narrow-ridge existence where we seek to discover which risks we take reinforce relationships with ourselves, others and with God, and which are destructive.

Locating my inner walls is of great importance. They are like the wing dams that the Army Corps of Engineers has constructed along the main channel of the Mississippi. These wing dams play an important role in keeping the channel open and regulating the depth of that passageway for barges and large boats. People could not have large boats on the Mississippi except for these structures. But they also need to know exactly where they are, for these same wing dams have destroyed the boats of those who did not take the time to know their location.

Acknowledging and owning my inner walls is a matter of personal integrity. It is a matter of attentiveness to my life and of honesty in admitting to myself what I see. Knowing that I need time and space in relationship to a person, and then providing it, is a way to tend carefully something important to me. Allowing myself the regenerative time for which only I can make provision is a way of caring deeply for those who need or want some of that time. Observing and accepting even those walls which are not life-giving is one important step in their eventual removal.

A friend sent me a poem whose author was not acknowledged in the newspaper where she found it. The poem offers some insights:

> Fences are
> and maybe they must be (i guess)
> some all around
> some just between
>   but if so

i like them airy enough
    to see through
and maybe low enough
    to climb over
or at least funny enough
    to just laugh at.
Fences without fun
    are cages.

Inner walls are removed the same way they are set, and they are set in much the same way the stone fences in New England are—stone by stone. The difference between our inner walls and the stone ones is that when we carry one stone after another to make the wall, we are aware of both our effort and its building. Life would be less complicated if we were as aware of our inner working as we are of our outer activity.

One thing is certain. If I am a person who either by instinct or by choice closes doors before I have looked through them; seeks security from being hurt as my highest priority; believes that avoiding mistakes in relationships is a value above all others; is unwilling to let people know that I care for them for fear of rejection, I will certainly become the best of all possible safety-first people. I will then have to take the credit for choosing to be not lonely, but isolated and eventually alienated even from myself.

Jesus and walls

There are good human reasons why the letter to the Ephesians says that Jesus is "the peace between us," that it is he who can best break down the walls that separate us. Jesus was neither an instinctive self-protector nor was he a security seeker. All of Jesus' life, and most especially his relationships with others, gives witness to the costly invitation that following him and being like him asks of us.

Jesus was the object of bitter criticism from his enemies and from those not courageous enough to follow him. His continual association with the marginal types of his time—dining with tax collectors, being touched and anointed by a woman of the street—made Jesus no favorite in the eyes of the legalists and the no-risk righteous ones.

His words that we must be willing to lose our lives in order to find them speak exactly to the heart of our ways of relating to ourselves and to others and so to God. It is difficult for us to develop in our own lives his way of living. So too it is difficult to cultivate so deeply our place of reflection and prayer that we can risk all, even to the point of what others might judge folly, yet without embracing the self-destructive in us. Knowing the difference is a matter of the truest kind of inner freedom linked with a willingness to take responsibility for what we say and do.

Jesus was a pleaser only in relationship to God whom he called Father. He prized acceptability above all other values only when he came before that same Father. His price was the loneliness of one whose freedom and inner integrity have grown together in such a way that all else flows out of them.

Jesus could approach the life of the saint and the sinner, the faith-filled and the nonbeliever, the honest and the lying, the pillars of his society and the outcasts, and be sensitively present to each. People left him with a greater knowledge of exactly who they were but without discouragement and without hopelessness. Those who wanted to follow his dream to have "life to the full" were sure of the loving invitation he offered.

This made Jesus a defenseless person before his enemies. It made him a person always vulnerable to those who would seek to distort both the truth of his words and the message of his personal life.

We look to him as we deal with our inner geography. In

relationship to the message of his life we can hope for the strong help we need as we seek to rid our lives of barriers of hostility and of protectiveness. Then the life that can only come to us through sharing life with others will find its way into our otherwise lonely lives.

XI
Making the word flesh in our lives

He humbled you, he made you feel hunger, he fed you with manna which neither you nor your fathers had known, to make you understand that man does not live on bread alone but that man lives on everything that comes from the mouth of Yahweh.

Deuteronomy 8:3

I am a person who has often lived lonely in my own human skin. The loneliness I feel is sometimes like being a foreigner to myself. At other times I feel like a stranger even to the people I love the most. It is a feeling that has continually challenged me to search for the meaning of my life; it is a feeling that has made me keenly aware that my own fragile life needs nourishing food.

Because of this, perhaps more than anything else, I have been led to pursue the meaning of the presence of the risen Jesus in the Eucharist. Because of this, I approach the table with a sense of my need to be nourished and the realization that it is a place to be involved in sharing life. It is not as simple as my first holy communion understanding of what receiving Jesus meant to me, yet it is not unrelated to that.

As I review the meaning of the Eucharist in my life, I must begin with my first eucharistic community—my family. Without theorizing about it, we instinctively understood the meaning of Eucharist and the Last Supper to be a reflection and a continuation of all the other meals Jesus shared with friends.

When the ten of us gathered, especially for the celebration of Sunday dinner, those meals had meaning because we were sharing the bread of our lives through every day of the week. They had meaning because we listened to the word of each other's lives. They had meaning because my father and mother knew what it meant to be body broken and given, and blood poured out and shared with others. Theirs was not a theoretical understanding of what it means to share who one is.

I experienced more of the Eucharist in my home than I could understand as a child. It is only in the past several years, especially as I have struggled to reach across death to experience the presence of my parents still with me, that I have understood the meaning of the presence of the risen Christ in every breaking of the bread.

As I review the meaning of the Eucharist for my life, I think of the family and eucharistic community to which I belong as a Franciscan Sister of Perpetual Adoration. It is a gift for me that my religious community is centered in one of the mysteries of the Christian experience—the Eucharist.

It is our gift to be challenged to deepen our understanding of Christ present to us and not lose the meaning of the meals shared at each table—in the chapel and in the dining room. To lose the meaning of table fellowship would be to misunderstand the reserved presence in our adoration chapel.

This has challenged my religious community to listen carefully to the word of God and the teaching of the church about the mystery of Christ's presence both at the table and in the reserved presence. This listening has had its own costly but redeeming pain. It has been a life-giving search that has deepened our commitment and challenged each of us to enflesh the meaning of Eucharist in our lives. The journey that began with my family continues in the journey of my community.

That journey continues for me now in a city in which I

find myself walking with some unusual companions, a city in which the bread of many human lives is broken daily.

Each day as I walk to work, first down Beacon Street and then along the edge of the Public Garden and up the hill into the Boston Common, I am dramatically confronted with the brokenness of human lives. I am continually reminded of the haunting questions, "What did it mean for Jesus and what must it mean for me to be a body broken for others, and to offer my life poured out in the act of sharing life?"

When it is warm, the benches along the edge of both the Garden and the Common are filled with people sleeping, face upward. They are vulnerable to life even in their moments of sleep. As I look at those faces, sometimes feeling as though I am invading their sacred need for privacy, I wonder why it is that they are sleeping and I am walking. I wonder how it was that the word of their lives was not one of a hope strong enough to sustain them. I wonder why they let go of or walked away from life in the wake of the same circumstances that cause others to catch hold of their lives.

These questions pursue and haunt me as I continue my walk. They are with me, again, as I go into a chapel for the noon liturgy and discover some of those same faces present in the congregation.

Then, when we approach to receive the bread and to take the cup, I notice the faces again. I wonder if they lost hope because there was no one there to reach to them or because the hand that reached to them did not offer enough of the promise of life. Why didn't the bread they now receive nourish them as they received it through their lives? Was there no one there to offer them the faithful message of God's love? Was there no one there to proclaim the word of God with conviction? Did no one announce with credibility and hope that the bread cannot nourish unless the word has first taken root in our lives? Why have we, like them, not taken more seriously the words of Jesus: "Man does not live by bread alone but on every word that comes forth from the mouth of God"? Why have we failed to understand that, unless and until we have allowed the word into our lives, we are like the Syrophoenician woman?

> But the woman had come up and was kneeling at his feet. "Lord," she said, "help me." He replied, "It is not fair to take the children's food and throw it to the house-dogs."
>
> Matthew 15:25-26

Bread that is broken and eaten apart from the breaking open of God's word is like the bread given to these dogs. If the words seem harsh, it is because of our serious responsibility to be implicated in the meaning of the word if we would do as Jesus demanded, namely, become the bread we break and eat in each Eucharist.

In our eagerness to receive the bread, we have either forgotten or failed to take notice of the clear message in both the Hebrew scriptures and in the words of Jesus:

> "See what days are coming—it is the Lord Yahweh who speaks—days when I will bring famine on the country, a famine not of bread, a drought not of water, but of the hearing of the word of Yahweh."
>
> Amos: 8:11

Morris West in *The Clowns of God* says that our failure to understand the message of the gospel lies in our propensity to try and explain the ways of God to men and women. West suggests that we can never explain God's ways and that we ought simply to announce God's coming into our lives, announce that news with inner integrity and with openness to life. When the word of God is announced in that way, then God explains himself to those who hear. And when they have heard the word proclaimed so that it can take root, the bread broken becomes for us the Bread of Life.

The presence of the street people in my city, in my life and at the table of the Eucharist, invites me to think back to the first Followers of the Way, the earliest communities to break the bread and share the cup according to the words of Jesus. To remember and act according to the marks which characterized these communities is a way of rooting ourselves in the possibility of being faithful to the meaning of both the word that we hear and the bread that we receive. We understand the meaning of neither if we try to separate them.

Characteristics of the earliest eucharistic communities

The earliest Followers of the Way came to follow Jesus through the sensitivity and wisdom of his words. They found meaning in their lives as they listened to his stories and parables about the simple and down-to-earth realities of their day-to-day life. So sacred were the words of Jesus that some members of the community wrote them down to preserve them for those who would follow.

The earliest Followers of the Way knew that the meaning of the Last Supper did not begin with preparations for the celebration of this Passover meal. Its meaning had grown and been realized through all of the meals that Jesus shared with friends.

The earliest Followers of the Way came together in shared admiration and love for this Jesus who continually reminded them that he wanted others to recognize his followers not by their love for him but through sharing with and giving love to each other.

The earliest Followers of the Way heard in Jesus' words and saw in the example of his daily life that suffering and loneliness will be the companion of every person who cares enough to live by his teaching and to tell others about it.

The earliest Followers of the Way had often heard and seen that following Jesus would make them neither popular

nor keep them safe from harm. His was the costly invitation to live close to the message of life if they were to realize his dream of "life to the full."

Jesus, by the example of his own life in the calling of his disciples and closest followers, proclaimed that there is not full life in isolation. Jesus knew from his human experience that we cannot claim and cling to values unless we have someone with whom to share them. He called us to be a people who live in relationship to one another. Realizing that our own strength is not enough if we catch hold of and claim his values, we are called to share what we are and have, to enter into the fullness of the table of friendship. We speak of table fellowship as one of the characteristics of both the earliest and the present eucharistic communities.

The earliest Followers of the Way saw how Jesus lived and they heard his words of life for them. In both they discovered that Jesus calls us not only to share with one another but to serve and care for each other. Jesus proclaimed this message clearly in his conversation with Peter:

> After the meal Jesus said to Simon Peter, "Simon son of John, do you love me more than these others do?" He answered, "Yes Lord, you know I love you." Jesus said to him, "Feed my lambs." A second time he said to him, "Simon son of John, do you love me?" He replied, "Yes, Lord, you know I love you." Jesus said to him, "Look after my sheep." Then he said to him a third time, "Simon son of John, do you love me?" Peter was upset that he asked him the third time, "Do you love me?" and said, "Lord, you know everything; you know I love you." Jesus said to him, "Feed my sheep. . . ."
>
> John 21:15-17

We cannot claim to be faithful eucharistic communities unless we make the same commitment as the early followers to assume the stance of Jesus when he washed the feet of the apostles at that last meal and when he said, "I stand in your midst as one committed to the service of others." Our understanding of what it means is possible only if we have a firm commitment to enfleshing the word in our daily lives. Even in the stories told by the writers of the gospel, we observe a Jesus who spoke to the crowds and shared the meaning of his life with them before he broke bread with them. We remember the words of the disciples on the road to Emmaus, "Did not our hearts burn as he talked to us on the road and explained the scriptures to us?" (Lk 24:32)

Just as service and feeding became synonymous for the earliest Followers of the Way, so it was clear to them that they were called to reach out to share what they had received. Their mission was to live according to Jesus' life and teaching so that they could lead others to embrace the same way of life. It remains our mission today.

If we faithfully follow these marks, they will transform us into the bread we eat in Eucharist. When we are faithful as were the early Followers of the Way, then certain characteristics will emerge in us and in our communities that will better insure our ability to invite, nourish and sustain those who are poor and powerless, those who are seeing yet sightless when they read the word. And having proclaimed the word faithfully, we share the bread that we have become.

Characteristics of eucharistic communities today

In faithfulness to the message of the earliest followers, and in faithfulness to themselves, today's eucharistic communities are called to service and to be in mission. To be faithful in this way requires several attributes.

A listening stance toward life. Without this neither the community nor the individual will have a heart like a well-prepared field at the time of planting—ready to receive the word of God. Only through carefully listening to our lives and to God's word can we discover God's way for us. Because of this Jesus said to those who would be his followers: "It is not those who say to me, 'Lord, Lord,' who will enter the kingdom of heaven, but the person who does the will of my father in heaven" (Mt 7:21). To further clarify what it is that separates the faithful follower from one who refuses to follow or follows at a distance, Jesus reminds them:

> "Therefore, everyone who listens to these words and acts on them will be like a sensible man who built his house on rock. Rain came down, floods rose, gales blew and hurled themselves against the house, and it did not fall: it was founded on rock. But everyone who listens to these words of mine and does not act on them will be like a stupid man who built his house on sand. Rain came down, floods rose, gales blew and struck that house, and it fell: and what a fall it had!"
>
> Matthew 7:24-27

An awareness that it is God who calls us to life. Few themes are more frequently repeated so clearly than God's continual call and our ever-present opportunity to respond to that call. The call to life comes through the word. The strength to respond is rooted in that nourishing word. It is a part of God's promise to us.

> Yes, as the rain and the snow come down from the heavens and do not return without watering the earth, making it yield and giving growth to provide seed for the sower and bread for the eating, so the word that goes from my mouth does not return to me empty, without carrying out my will and succeeding in what it was sent to do.
>
> Isaiah 55:10-11

An admission of our emptiness needing to be filled. The biblical concept of being filled begins in our hunger. Heaven is portrayed as a banquet place; conversion as a turning away from our inner hunger to allow God to feed us. We must first empty ourselves so that we can receive the food that nourishes. Conversion is not so much a matter of asking

God to remove our hunger as it is to allow ourselves to be filled by that same God. This is the hunger we bring to the table of the Eucharist. Accepting our own hunger can only grow out of receiving the meaning of the word.

A sense of our sinfulness in need of reconciliation. St. Paul makes it abundantly clear that it is only by God's gift that we are invited to live, only through God's tender mercy are we repeatedly called back to the way of life. God has so empowered the word that it is possible for us to offer our sinfulness to him as an acceptable sacrifice through which we receive forgiveness and an invitation to discover new and richer life.

Making the Eucharist a way of life. Knowing the cost of becoming bread is the beginning of an inner desire to make the Eucharist not something that we share but something that we are. Knowing the cost of becoming that bread begins in our loneliness, in our sense of our great hunger and our emptiness waiting to be filled. It begins when this is acknowledged before God and in the companionship of those who journey with us. Accepting the cost of becoming bread invites us to share the powerless and unblessed in us so that it may be transformed into God's own strength and gracious life. When we nourish our desire to become the Eucharist which we share, we experience the sacred connections between ourselves and God in a faithful way that continues to reach to others.

A commitment to make the word flesh in our lives. The first five attributes are important in preparing our hearts and our lives for this final and most important one. We are reminded in Deuteronomy, "He humbled you, he made you feel hunger," and again in Amos, "I will bring a famine on the country, not of bread but of the hearing of the word of Yahweh." We remember that the same God who calls us to become the word made flesh like Jesus instills in us a hunger for the meaning of that word. The same God who promises food and then provides it reminds us that we cannot walk without soon growing weary if we approach the table with hearts and minds empty because the meaning of and commitment to the word is not present in us.

Becoming the bread

As I continue to make my own inner journey, seeking to be nourished first by the word so that I become the bread, the reminder of the street people continues to haunt me. I am pursued by the desire to share the word and to offer the bread in whatever way I have become one with it. I am also pursued with the question of how the clear words of Jesus have been so obscured even by those who say they wish to be faithful. I wonder why we continue to try to explain the word rather than to proclaim it with our lives. I wonder why we make mockery of the bread when we continue to approach the table with little or no accountability for our lack of involvement in the word. The word demands that we remember that community is not complete until it is envisioned as world community, that our service is self-serving when it is selective and exclusive, that our sense of mission must be like that of the first disciples whom Jesus told to "Go teach and be present to all nations" (Mt 28:20).

In speaking at the 42nd International Eucharistic Congress, Cardinal Pablo Munoz Vega spoke of how the word and the bread must be present when he said, "As a condition for being authentic today, Catholicism must present itself as action, as a historical initiative taken toward a more just and human society." In speaking of how this can be he said:

> Nothing is missing in the idea of justice, freedom and peace
> which Jesus Christ entrusted to us in his living word and
> in the apostolic magisterium; absolutely nothing is missing
> or needs to be updated by other ideas. . . . The light and

life necessary for our world in crisis are integrally present in it. All that is outside it lacks the strength afforded by its "cornerstone," and is superficial and vain.[1]

Part of the loneliness of my journey has been the need for me to grow beyond my "first holy communion" understanding of almost everything that I believe. It has set me in search of those who could be present to me and speak to me words that are a part of God's word because, like it, they challenge me to discover the difference between food that nourishes and empty promises that will never fill. They cannot be fulfilled in a way that is faithful to the life to which God calls us.

Judy Collins sang of this relationship between the word that speaks of meaning and the food that nourishes that meaning when she sang, "Our lives will not be sweated from birth until life closes; Hearts starve as well as bodies, Bread and roses. Bread and roses . . ." but Edna St. Vincent Millay has the final word here:

> I must not die of pity; I must live;
> Grow strong, not sicken; eat, digest my food,
> That it may build me, and in doing good
> To blood and bone, broaden the sensitive
> fastidious perception: we contrive
> Lean comfort for the starving, who intrude
> Upon them with our pots of pity; brewed
> From stronger meat must be the broth we give.
>
> .   .   .
>
> If I would help the weak, I must be fed
> In wit and purpose, pour away despair
> And rinse the cup, eat happiness like bread.[2]

---

1. *Origins,* August 27, 1981, Vol. II, No. 11.
2. Collected Poems, Edna St. Vincent Millay (New York: Harper & Row, Paperback edition).